# The Women's Movement

AMERICAN VOICES FROM

# The Women's Movement

Virginia Schomp

**Marshall Cavendish**
Benchmark
New York

# TO "CUZ" MARIAN SCHOMP

Marshall Cavendish Benchmark
99 White Plains Road
Tarrytown, New York 10591-9001
www.marshallcavendish.us

Text copyright © 2007 by Marshall Cavendish Corporation

*Library of Congress Cataloging-in-Publication Data*
Schomp, Virginia.
The women's movement / by Virginia Schomp.
p. cm. — (American voices from)
Summary: "Describes the history of the women's rights movement in the United States, from colonial times to the present day, through the use of primary sources such as letters, diary entries, official government documents, newspaper articles, historical art, and photographs"—Provided by publisher.
Includes bibliographical references and index.
ISBN-13: 978-0-7614-2171-9
ISBN-10: 0-7614-2171-8
1. Feminism—United States—History—Juvenile literature. 2. Feminism—United States—History—Sources. 3. Women's rights—United States—History—Juvenile literature.
4. Women's rights—United States—History—Sources. I. Title.
HQ1410.S275 2006      305.420973—dc22
2006005800

Printed in Malaysia
1  3  5  6  4  2

Editor: Joyce Stanton
Editorial Director: Michelle Bisson
Art Director: Anahid Hamparian
Series design and composition: Anne Scatto / PIXEL PRESS

*Images provided by Art Editor Rose Corbett Gordon and Alexandra Gordon, Mystic CT, from the following sources:*

Cover: Charles Gatewood/The Image Works
Pages ii, xiii, 4, 36, 54, 83, 90 top, 98, 112, 114, 117, 131: Bettmann/Corbis; pages viii, xviii, 39, 40, 93: Time & Life Pictures/Getty Images; pages x, xiv, xvi, 5, 11, 19, 24, 32, 47, 50, 60, 67, 69, 76, 87 top, 97, 128, 130 top, 130 bottom: Hulton Archive/Getty Images; page xi: Susan W. & Stephen C. Paine Collection; page xii: Getty Images; pages xvii, 27, 53, 57, 87 bottom, 129 top: Corbis; pages xx, 21 top, 21 bottom: North Wind Picture Archives; page 2: The Newark Museum/Art Resource, NY; page 7: The Granger Collection, NY; page 13: National Portrait Gallery, Smithsonian/Art Resource, NY; pages 17, 129 bottom: The Art Archive/Culver Pictures; page 26 left: Corporation of London/Topham-HIP/The Image Works; page 26 right: Mary Evans Picture Library/The Image Works; page 30: American Textile History Museum, Lowell, Massachusetts; page 42: Musée de la Ville de Paris, Musee Carnavalet, Paris/Giraudon/Bridgeman Art Library; page 61: Photri/Topham/The Image Works; page 64: ANA/ The Image Works; page 66: Smithsonian Institution, Warshaw Collection of Business Americana; page 71: Roger-Viollet/ Topham/ The Image Works; page 75: Library of Congress; page 81: Minnesota Historical Society/Corbis; page 90 bottom: Elliott Erwitt/Magnum Photos; page 94: Marc Riboud/ Magnum Photos; page 102: Charles Gatewood/The Image Works; page 104: Jesse-Steve Rose/The Image Works; page 107: JP Laffont/Sygma/Corbis; page 108: Michael Okoniewski/The Image Works; page 115: AFP/Getty Images; page 120: Tom & Dee Ann McCarthy/Corbis; page 122: Micheline Pelletier/Corbis Sygma; page 123: Strauss/Curtis/Corbis.

ON THE COVER: A "women's liberation" rally in New York City, 1970.

ON THE TITLE PAGE: Twelve-year-old Maria Pepe's lawsuit against Little League forced the organization to allow girls to play.

# Acknowledgments

Abigail Adams to John Adams, March 31, 1776; and John Adams to Abigail Adams, April 14, 1776, from L. H. Butterfield and others, editors. *Adams Family Correspondence.* Vol. 1. Cambridge, MA: Harvard University Press, 1963. Used by permission of Massachusetts Historical Society.

Emma Willard, *An Address to the Public; Particularly to the Members of the Legislature of New-York, Proposing a Plan for Improving Female Education.* Middlebury, NY: J. W. Copeland, 1819. Used by permission of Emma Willard School, Troy, New York.

"Why Women Want to Vote" flyer, National American Woman Suffrage Association, May 10, 1910. Courtesy of the Library of Congress.

Margaret Sanger, "Why I Went to Jail," *Together,* February 1960, from the Papers of Margaret Sanger, Library of Congress.

*Shipyard Diary of a Woman Welder* by Augusta Clawson, illustrated by Boris Givotovsky, copyright 1944 by Penguin Books Inc. Used by permission of Viking Penguin, a division of Penguin Group (USA) Inc.

Betty Friedan, *The Feminine Mystique.* New York: W. W. Norton, 1963, 1974. Copyright © 1963, 1964, 1966, 1970, 1971, 1972, 1973, 1974, 1975, 1976, 1985, 1991, 1998 by Betty Friedan. Reprinted by courtesy of Curtis Brown, Ltd.

Jayne West, "Are Men Really the Enemy" quiz, and the *Redstockings Manifesto,* July 7, 1969; from Rosalyn Baxandall and Linda Gordon, editors, *Dear Sisters: Dispatches from the Women's Liberation Movement.* New York: Basic Books, 2000.

Excerpts from *The Phyllis Schlafly Report* 6 (November 1972) by Phyllis Schlafly. Used by permission of Phyllis Schlafly.

"The Wage Gap Over Time: In Real Dollars, Women See a Continuing Gap," ©2004 National Committee on Pay Equity. Reprinted by permission of National Committee on Pay Equity.

*Taking the Lead: Girls' Rights in the 21st Century,* a nationwide survey of school-age children conducted for Girls Incorporated® by Harris Interactive, Inc. © 2000 Girls Incorporated. Used by permission of Girls Incorporated.

# Contents

This glimpse of a lady's underclothes would have been scandalous in 1895!

# About Primary Sources

## What Is a Primary Source?

In the pages that follow, you will be hearing many different "voices" from an exciting chapter in American history. Some of the selections are long and others are short. You will find many easy to understand, while others may require several readings. All the selections have one thing in common, however. They are primary sources. This is the name historians give to the bits and pieces of information that make up the record of human existence. Primary sources are important to us because they are the core material of all historical investigation. You might call them "history" itself.

Primary sources are evidence. They give historians the facts and clues they need to understand the past. Perhaps you have read a detective story in which an investigator must solve a mystery by uncovering and piecing together bits of evidence. The detective makes deductions, or educated guesses, based on the evidence. When all the deductions point in the same direction, the mystery is solved. Historians work in much the same way. Like detectives, they analyze data through careful reading and rereading. They question and

The creator of this cartoon, most certainly a male, takes a poke at women who wear "bloomers." The loose trousers, worn under skirts, were popular for a while in the nineteenth century.

compare sources. After much analysis, they draw conclusions about an event, a person, or an entire era. Different historians may analyze the same evidence and come to different conclusions. That is why there is often sharp disagreement about an event.

Primary sources are also called *documents*. This rather dry word can be used to describe many different things: an official speech by a government leader, an act of Congress, an old map, a letter worn out from much handling, an entry scrawled in a diary, a newspaper article, a funny or sad song, a colorful poster, a cartoon, a faded photograph, or someone's remembrances captured on tape or film.

By examining the following documents, you, the reader, will be taking on the role of historian. Here is your chance to immerse yourself in one of the great social movements in American history: the women's rights movement. You will hear the voices of women who have protested their inferior status in American society from colonial times to the present day. You will share the experiences of female abolitionists who defied tradition by speaking out against slavery, suffragists who fought for women's right to vote, and pioneers in education, labor, birth control, and other reforms. You will meet the "second-wave feminists" of the turbulent 1960s and 1970s and young women confronting continued sex discrimination today. You will also hear from the opposition—Americans who through the centuries have responded to the long struggle for women's rights with anger, outrage, and ridicule.

## How to Read a Primary Source

This book tells the story of the American women's movement through historical documents. These include newspaper accounts

This advertisement for electric typewriters was published around 1900. Secretarial work was one of the few "respectable" jobs open to middle-class women at the time.

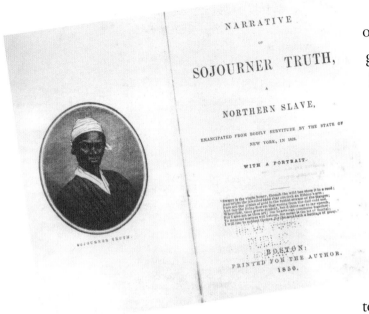

NARRATIVE
of
SOJOURNER TRUTH,

A

NORTHERN SLAVE,

EMANCIPATED FROM BODILY SERVITUDE BY THE STATE OF
NEW YORK, IN 1828.

WITH A PORTRAIT.

BOSTON:
PRINTED FOR THE AUTHOR.
1850.

Former slave Sojourner Truth left behind a written record of her life in "bodily servitude." After gaining her freedom, she became a leader of the early women's rights movement.

of feminist activities and government records of legal reforms. There are speeches, declarations, and letters from leaders of the women's movement. You will also find some writings and remembrances by the "forgotten" women who waged the day-to-day battle for women's rights in many areas of American society. Most of the selections are by women, but a few reflect the sentiments of men on both sides of the debate.

As you read each document, ask yourself some basic questions. Who is writing or speaking? What is the writer's point of view? Who is that person's audience? What is she or he trying to tell the audience? Is the message clearly expressed or is it implied, that is, stated indirectly? What words does the writer use to convey the message? Are the words emotional or objective in tone? If you are looking at a photograph, examine it carefully, taking in all the details. Where do you think it was taken? What is happening in the foreground? In the background? Is it posed or an action shot? How can you tell? Who do you think took the picture, and what is its purpose? These are questions that can help you think critically about a primary source.

A few tools have been included with the documents to help you in your investigations. Unusual words are defined near the selections or in the glossary at the back of the book. Thought-provoking questions follow each document. You'll probably come up with many questions of your own. That's great! The work of a historian always leads to many, many questions. Some can be answered, while others require more investigation. Perhaps when you finish this book, you'll have questions of your own that will lead you to further explorations of the American women's movement.

Political activist Phyllis Schlafly led a backlash against the women's movement in the 1970s.

A "suffragette" campaigns for women's
voting rights in the early 1900s.

# Introduction

## A TIDAL WAVE

It is hard to imagine a time when it was illegal for an American woman to vote. Not so long ago, state and federal laws discriminated against women, restricting their freedom to participate in politics, own property, earn a living, or control their own wages. Laws and traditions maintained that women were intellectually inferior to men. The only proper place for a woman, many people believed, was in the "private sphere" of home and family.

From the beginnings of American history, there have been brave women who have struggled to break down those barriers. Their campaign for equality has seen both bitter disappointments and extraordinary victories. It has brought about deep and lasting changes in the nation's political, legal, economic, and educational systems. Over time the women's rights movement has transformed American society, challenging many of our most basic beliefs, customs, and institutions.

There have been two major periods of intense activity during the long struggle for women's rights.

The "first wave" began in 1848, when a handful of activists led by Elizabeth Cady Stanton organized the first women's rights convention. Most of the women who attended this historic meeting in Seneca Falls, New York, were volunteers in abolition and other social reform movements. Through their work in reform, they had become more aware of their own strengths and abilities. They had also been frustrated by the rules limiting women's participation in public life. The Declaration of Sentiments adopted at the Seneca Falls convention called for an end to women's social and legal inequality, and it inspired a movement dedicated to fighting for that cause.

Abolitionist Lucy Stone was one of the "founding mothers" of the women's rights movement.

Early activists in the women's movement worked for a variety of reforms: liberalized property and divorce laws, greater educational opportunities, better conditions for factory workers, an end to child labor. Arguments over which issues deserved the most attention sometimes caused bitter divisions within the ranks. By the early twentieth century, however, most feminists had united behind a single issue—suffrage, or the right to vote. In 1920, with the ratification of the Nineteenth Amendment to the Constitution, women finally won that right.

Some feminists believed that winning the vote meant the end of their struggle for equality. For several decades the women's movement fell relatively quiet, drained of much of its energy and influence. Meanwhile, society was changing. Millions of women entered the workforce, especially during World War II and after the war's end in 1945. As they ventured outside their traditional roles, these women discovered new choices and freedoms. At the same time, they encountered disturbing evidence of continued discrimination.

The 1960s ushered in a period of social upheaval. Americans began to challenge racial prejudice and many other aspects of society. Young people rebelled against the older generation's traditional customs and values. Antiwar demonstrators protested U.S. military involvement in Vietnam. In the midst of these turbulent times, the second wave of the women's movement was born.

During World War II, millions of American women took jobs traditionally held by men.

Policewomen arrest a civil rights protester in the 1960s.

Many modern feminists got their first taste of political activism in civil rights marches and anti-war demonstrations. The widespread calls for social reform and protests against oppression made them more aware of their own second-class status. Like the women abolitionists of the nineteenth century, second-wave feminists brought their newfound awareness to a campaign for women's rights.

Twentieth-century feminists worked for advances in areas including equal opportunities in employment and education, equal treatment under the law, and reproductive choices. They achieved many successes. But like the earlier feminists, the women of the second wave often divided over goals and tactics. And when the nation entered a more conservative period in the 1980s, these women, too, left much work unfinished.

Today a number of the women's organizations formed in the 1960s and 1970s remain active. Groups such as the National Organization for Women continue to work for women's rights in the workplace, schools, on the streets, and in the courts. Members of these organizations include both "graying" feminists and a younger generation of women sometimes referred to as "third wavers."

Some feminists object to dividing the history of the women's movement into waves. They argue that American women of all classes and races have worked tirelessly for more than two centuries to end discrimination and achieve full equality. As we hear the words of these often-forgotten crusaders, we come face-to-face with what feminist writer Robin Morgan has called the "buried history of activism." Their stories, along with the writings and reflections of their better-known sisters, are evidence that the women's movement flowed continuously over the centuries and has never really ended. "Actually," says Morgan, "today's Women's Movement is more like 'the ten thousandth wave'—a *tidal* wave—that keeps on rolling."

A colonial woman finds time to read while working at her spinning wheel.

# Chapter I

# A Woman's Place

**F**OR EARLY EUROPEAN SETTLERS in America, life was an endless battle for survival. As they carved out new homes from the wilderness, the colonists faced starvation, disease, bitter cold, and backbreaking labor. Men and women shared the hardships. The men cleared the land, plowed, planted, chopped wood, built homes, and hunted. Women cared for the children and ran the households, producing nearly all the goods their families needed—bread, butter, soap, candles, clothing, medicines. Many farm women helped plant and harvest the crops and tend the livestock. In growing towns wives often worked alongside their husbands in businesses such as blacksmithing, shoemaking, or innkeeping.

Although their work was vital and highly respected, colonial women were not granted the same rights as men. American legal codes were based on English common law, an unwritten body of laws under which women gave up their separate legal identity when they married. A married woman's wages and property belonged to her husband. She could not buy or sell property, sign a contract, sue in court, or make a will without his consent. If a couple separated, the man automatically had custody of the children. American laws also prohibited both married and single women from serving on a jury or voting.

Traditional ideas and attitudes enforced women's second-class status. Most colonists were devout Christians. In church they learned that God had made women inferior in mind and body as a punishment for Eve's sins in the Garden of Eden. A woman's place, they were told, was in the home. Her proper role was that of wife and mother. Married women were expected to obey their husbands, in accordance with biblical commands such as, "Wives, submit yourselves unto your own husband, as unto the Lord."

Colonial women had few educa-

English-born artist John Wollaston painted this portrait of a contented American family in the mid-1700s.

tional opportunities. While boys might study math or science, most girls were taught little more than reading, writing, and the skills needed to care for a home and family. Instead of "ruining their minds" with books, they were urged to work on strengthening their "natural" virtues of meekness, modesty, compassion, obedience, purity, and religious devotion. A popular journal called *The Married Lady's Companion* advised wives "to adapt yourself to your husband, whatever may be his peculiarities. Nature has made man the stronger, [and] the consent of mankind has given him superiority over his wife. . . . You ought to cultivate a cheerful and happy submission."

Not everyone submitted meekly to these restrictions. From early colonial times there were strong-willed women who challenged society and demanded the right to think for themselves. But women did not begin to work together for a common cause until the American Revolution.

The Revolution was founded on principles of liberty and equality. Thousands of colonial women embraced those Patriot ideals, working tirelessly for independence. They organized boycotts of British goods and made their families' clothes from rough homespun instead of imported materials. They raised funds and donated supplies to George Washington's ragged army. Some women served the army as cooks, laundresses, spies, scouts, and nurses. Others toiled on the home front. While their menfolk fought, women on each side—both Patriots and Loyalists (those who remained loyal to Britain)—managed the homes, farms, and businesses.

Some colonial women went even further. They risked their lives fighting as Revolutionary soldiers. In April 1775 the women of Groton, Massachusetts, dressed in their husbands' clothes, armed

A young Patriot loads a musket during the American Revolution.

themselves with muskets and pitchforks, and set out to defend the bridge leading into town. The women succeeded in capturing a British officer who was carrying valuable military intelligence. Similar incidents occurred frequently during the course of the war. In addition, some women disguised themselves as men and enlisted in the Continental Army, while others fought alongside their husbands on the battlefield.

The American Revolution ended with the formation of a new republic. But the distance between the Revolutionary ideals and the reality of women's status caused some women to begin questioning their proper place in society. The Declaration of Independence had declared that all men were endowed "with certain unalienable rights." Why not women, too?

## Abigail Adams Asks, "Remember the Ladies"

Like many colonial women, Abigail Adams never attended school. On her own, however, this sharp-witted woman from Massachusetts taught herself to read and write English and French and became an avid student of history. In 1764 Abigail married John Adams. During and after the American Revolution, her husband played a leading role in the struggle for independence and the formation of the new republic. His duties called him away from home for months at a time. In his absence Abigail ran the household, raised four children, and managed the family's farm and business affairs. In 1776, as the all-male Continental Congress debated America's future, she sent this letter to John, asking that the new government consider the rights of women.

Future First Lady Abigail Adams believed that women deserved the same rights and opportunities as men.

MARCH 31 1776

I wish you would ever write me a Letter half as long as I write you. . . .

    I long to hear that you have declared an independancy—and by the way in the new Code of Laws which I suppose it will be necessary for you to make I desire you would Remember the Ladies, and be more generous and favourable to them than your ancestors. Do not put such unlimited power into the hands of the Husbands. Remember

*". . . all Men would be tyrants if they could."*

all Men would be tyrants if they could. If perticuliar care and attention is not paid to the Laidies we are determined to foment a Rebelion, and will not hold ourselves bound by any Laws in which we have no voice, or Representation.

That your Sex are Naturally Tyrannical is a Truth so thoroughly established as to admit of no dispute, but such of you as wish to be happy willingly give up the harsh title of Master for the more tender and endearing one of Friend. Why then, not put it out of the power of the vicious and the Lawless to use us with cruelty and indignity with impunity. Men of Sense in all Ages abhor those customs which treat us only as the vassals of your Sex. Regard us then as Beings placed by providence under your protection and in the immitation of the Supreem Being make use of that power only for our happiness.

*—From L. H. Butterfield and others, editors.* Adams Family Correspondence. *Vol. 1. Cambridge, MA: Harvard University Press, 1963.*

## THINK ABOUT THIS

1. How does Abigail describe men's nature?
2. Do you think Abigail is being playful, or "mock-serious," in some parts of this letter? If so, where? How can you tell?
3. How do you think Abigail would describe the ideal relationship between men and women?

## John Adams Defends "Our Masculine Systems"

As a delegate to the First and Second Continental Congresses and later as America's first vice president and second president, John Adams played a major role in transforming the colonies into an

During his long career as a lawyer and political leader, John Adams exchanged more than a thousand letters with his wife and "dear Partner," Abigail.

independent nation. Along with other Revolutionary leaders, he condemned injustice and "taxation without representation." Yet the Constitution adopted by the new nation ignored the rights of African Americans, Native Americans, and women. Slavery remained legal, citizens were free to spread across Native lands, and only white male property owners were allowed to vote. In his reply to Abigail's letter, John treated her plea for women's rights as a joke. To this Founding Father and other colonial men, it was simply obvious that women's proper place was in the home.

AP[RIL] 14. 1776

You justly complain of my short Letters, but the critical State of Things and the Multiplicity of Avocations must plead my Excuse. . . . As to Declarations of Independency, be patient. . . .

As to your extraordinary Code of Laws, I cannot but laugh. We have been told that our Struggle has loosened the bands of Government every where. That Children and Apprentices were disobedient—that schools and Colledges were grown turbulent—that Indians slighted their Guardians and Negroes grew insolent to their Masters. But your Letter was the first Intimation that another Tribe more numerous and powerfull than all the rest were grown discontented.—This is rather too coarse a Compliment but you are so saucy, I wont blot it out.

Depend upon it, We know better than to repeal our Masculine systems. Altho they are in full Force, you know they are little more than Theory. We dare not exert our Power in its full Latitude. We are obliged to go fair, and softly, and in Practice you know We are the subjects. We have only the Name of Masters, and rather than give up this, which would compleatly subject Us to the Despotism of the Peticoat, I hope General Washington, and all our brave Heroes would fight.

> *"Depend upon it, We know better than to repeal our Masculine systems."*

*—From L. H. Butterfield and others, editors.* Adams Family Correspondence. *Vol. 1. Cambridge, MA: Harvard University Press, 1963.*

## THINK ABOUT THIS

1. What reason does John Adams give for opposing Abigail's plea for greater rights?

2. In a letter to fellow statesman James Sullivan in May 1776, John wrote, "[Women's] delicacy renders them unfit for practice and experience in the great businesses of life. . . . Besides, their attention is so much engaged with the necessary nurture of their children, that nature has made them fittest for domestic cares." How do his reasons for opposing women's rights differ in the two letters? What might account for the difference?

# Chapter 2

# Women in the Abolition Movement

THE FIRST WOMEN'S RIGHTS MOVEMENT grew out of the campaign to end slavery.

Slavery in America dated back to early colonial times. This brutal institution gradually died out in the North, where it proved impractical in the region's factories and small farms. By 1830, however, there were more than two million slaves in the South, most toiling in misery in plantation fields. Opponents of slavery began to join together, demanding its immediate abolition. Antislavery societies were formed, and thousands of men and women, including both whites and free blacks, were drawn to the cause.

Abolitionists faced bitter, often violent opposition from Southern slaveholders and white Northerners who supported slavery. Angry mobs destroyed antislavery presses and attacked abolitionist speakers. Women abolitionists endured the same hardships as men, plus an added burden—opposition from people on both sides of the slavery issue who considered their participation in public life scandalous.

Most men still believed that women's only proper place was in the home. While some antislavery societies accepted female members,

Harriet Beecher Stowe *(seated in center)*,
author of the best-selling antislavery novel *Uncle Tom's Cabin*,
poses with a group of female abolitionists.

others excluded them or restricted them to behind-the-scenes roles. In response women began to form their own societies. These all-female groups started schools and libraries for free blacks, published pamphlets, circulated petitions, and organized fund-raisers and conventions. Lucretia Mott, Angelina and Sarah Grimké, and other female abolitionists defied tradition by making public speeches, not only to women's groups but also to mixed audiences of women and men.

The result was a storm of outrage. Newspapers called the women abolitionists unfeminine, unnatural, and immoral. Politicians denounced them in speeches, and ministers condemned them from the pulpit. In Boston an assembly of white and black women abolitionists touched off a riot. In Philadelphia an anti-abolitionist mob burned down a hall where a women's antislavery convention was meeting.

Incidents like these only inspired more women to join the anti-slavery cause. Confronted by criticism of their public roles, some women reformers also began to think about their own inequality. "We have given great offense on account of our womanhood, which seems to be as objectionable as our abolitionism," wrote Angelina Grimké. "We are willing to bear the brunt of the storm, if we can only be the means of making a break in that wall of public opinion which lies right in the way of woman's rights, true dignity, honor and usefulness."

## Philadelphia Women Form an Antislavery Society

In 1833 abolitionist leader William Lloyd Garrison invited fellow reformer Lucretia Mott to attend the founding of the American

Anti-Slavery Society in Philadelphia. Mott was a minister in the Quaker religion, which granted women an unusual degree of responsibility in church affairs. Although she did not think it would be proper to join the men signing the constitution of Garrison's new society, she did say a few "modest" words in support of the cause. A few days later, Mott and three women friends held their own meeting. Together they founded the Philadelphia Female Anti-Slavery Society. Soon dozens of women's abolitionist organizations were operating in cities and small towns throughout the North. Most of these groups followed the principles outlined in the Philadelphia society's constitution.

Lucretia Mott was a Quaker minister and dedicated abolitionist.

CONSTITUTION OF THE PHILADELPHIA FEMALE ANTI-SLAVERY SOCIETY

Whereas, more than two millions of our fellow countrymen, of these United States, are held in abject bondage; and whereas, we believe that slavery and prejudice against color are contrary to the laws of God, and to the principles of our far-famed Declaration of Independence, and recognising the right of the slave to immediate emancipation; we deem it our duty to manifest our abhorrence of the flagrant injustice and deep sin of slavery, by united and vigorous exertions for its speedy removal, and for the restoration of the people of color to their inalienable rights. For these purposes, we, the undersigned, agree to associate ourselves under the name of "THE PHILADELPHIA FEMALE ANTI-SLAVERY SOCIETY."

> "It is especially recommended that the members of this Society should entirely abstain from purchasing the products of slave labor."

*ARTICLE I.* The object of this Society shall be to collect and disseminate correct information of the character of slavery, and of the actual condition of the slaves and free people of color, for the purpose of inducing the community to adopt such measures, as may be in their power, to dispel the prejudice against the people of color, to improve their condition, and to bring about the speedy abolition of slavery.

*ARTICLE II.* Any female uniting in these views, and contributing to the funds, shall be a member of the Society.

*ARTICLE III.* The officers of the Society shall be a President, a Vice President, a Recording Secretary, a Corresponding Secretary, a Treasurer, and Librarian, who, with six other members, shall constitute a Board of Managers. . . .

*ARTICLE XII.* It is especially recommended that the members of this Society should entirely abstain from purchasing the products of slave labor, that we may be able consistently to plead the cause of our brethren in bonds.

—*From* Fourth Annual Report of the Philadelphia Female Anti-Slavery Society, January 11, 1838. *Philadelphia: Merrihew and Gunn, 1838. Reprinted in Judith Papachristou,* Women Together. *New York: Alfred A. Knopf, 1976.*

1. According to the document, what was the main object, or purpose, of the society? How was this expected to serve the cause of abolition?
2. Why does the constitution urge members not to buy products made from slave labor?

## A "Ladies' Fair" Raises Funds for the Cause

Women's societies needed money to support their abolitionist activities. One of their most effective fund-raising tools was the "ladies' fair." Women donated handmade articles such as needlework, baskets, jewelry, hats, and baked goods for sale at these events, often held at antislavery conventions or during the Christmas shopping season. Women's groups sometimes coordinated their moneymaking efforts. In 1840, for example, more than thirty-five different societies contributed articles to the Massachusetts Anti-Slavery Fair, raising two thousand dollars for the cause. The following account of an antislavery fair in 1836 appeared in William Lloyd Garrison's abolitionist newspaper, *The Liberator.*

THE PROPOSED ANTI-SLAVERY FAIR was held on Thursday, the 22nd of December. . . . Around the Hall was placed in large letters the motto: On this day did our Fathers *land* on the Rock of Freedom. Let us *stand* firmly on this Rock. . . .

There was great variety in the articles, and many of them were very handsome and tasteful. The ladies have ever regarded the pecuniary [financial] benefit derived from these sales as but *one* of several reasons in their favor. The main object is to keep the subject before the public eye, and by every innocent expedient [method] to promote perpetual discussion. . . .

To promote this favorite object, various mottoes and devices were stamped upon the article offered for sale. Bunches of [writing] quills bore the label, "Twenty-five Weapons for Abolitionists." On the wafer-boxes was written, "The doom of Slavery is *sealed*." On one side of the pen-wipers was inscribed, "Wipe out the blot of Slavery"; on the other, "Plead the cause with thy Pen." On some needle-books was printed, "May the use of our needles prick the consciences of slave-holders"; others were made in the form of small shoes, and on the soles was written, "Trample not on the Oppressed."

**wafer-boxes**
*boxes holding small sticky disks used for sealing letters*

**pen-wipers**
*cloths used for cleaning fountain pens*

—From The Liberator, *January 2, 1837. Reprinted in Judith Papachristou,* Women Together. *New York: Alfred A. Knopf, 1976.*

## THINK ABOUT THIS

1. According to the organizers, what were the two main goals of antislavery fairs?
2. What tactics of modern-day political campaigns are similar to the "innocent expedients" used to promote the abolitionists' cause?

## A Young Volunteer Goes Door-to-Door

Women's greatest contributions to the abolitionist cause came through their work in petition drives. Female volunteers went door-to-door collecting signatures on petitions urging Congress to take antislavery actions such as abolishing slavery in the District of Columbia and prohibiting its spread to the western territories. The work was physically and emotionally challenging. Women spent long days knocking on doors, asking strangers for support. They often met with scorn and disapproval, as described in this passage from the journal of a young volunteer whose name has been forgotten. Despite the difficulties, determined female abolitionists sent more than twice as many petitions to Congress as male volunteers. More than half of the signatures on those tens of thousands of documents were made by women who agreed to support the abolitionist cause.

A weary reformer goes door-to-door in support of the antislavery cause.

[A] WOMAN, WHOM WE MET at the door, didn't want to have any thing to do with any paper of the kind; while her husband shouted from his easy chair in the parlour, that *"they were all opposed there to ladies doing delicate business."* . . .

A certain Mr. —— met us at the door of his own house, and when we asked him if there were any ladies within who would like to sign such a petition, he answered in a very decided, contemptuous manner, "NO"— without even so much as asking them. He apparently belonged to that too numerous class of men who claim the right to "possess exclusive jurisdiction in all cases whatsoever" over their wives' consciences; so we left him, and wishing him a good evening, walked on.

At one place, the father hoped there was nobody in his house who would sign such a paper; it was an insult to the public to send such papers to Congress, and a very great imposition, altogether too bad, to send young people about in that manner, on such despicable business. When we told him that we did it from choice, because we thought it our duty to do what was in our power for the oppressed, he bade us begone and to mind and never bring *such a thing to his house again.* We disclaimed all intentions of insulting any one, and told him we only wished to give them an opportunity to do their duty. He followed us to the door and dismissed us with a great deal of good advice, saying, "It's none of your business, *galls,* and you'd better go *right straight home.*"

> *"At one place, the father hoped there was nobody in his house who would sign such a paper."*

*—From* The Liberator, *August 4, 1837. Reprinted in Judith Papachristou,* Women Together. *New York: Alfred A. Knopf, 1976.*

## THINK ABOUT THIS

1. What attitudes about women are displayed in the men's reactions to the petition workers?
2. What arguments would you have used to answer the critics?

## The Church Criticizes Independent Women

Sarah and Angelina Grimké grew up in South Carolina, in a well-to-do slaveholding family. As adults the two women moved to Philadelphia.

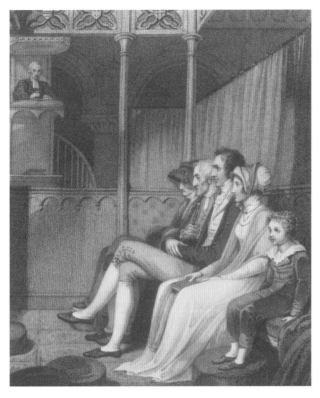

A family listens attentively to a church sermon. Early American church leaders were almost exclusively male and almost always opposed to women taking an active role outside the home.

Their firsthand knowledge of the horrors of slavery, along with their Quaker faith, inspired them to join the abolitionist cause. The sisters were brilliant speakers whose lectures attracted large audiences of both women and men. Their fame also inspired harsh disapproval. In 1837, when the Grimkés began a lecture tour of Massachusetts, leaders of the powerful Congregational Church issued a "pastoral letter" that was read from pulpits throughout the state.

## PASTORAL LETTER OF THE GENERAL ASSOCIATION OF MASSACHUSETTS TO THE CONGREGATIONAL CHURCHES UNDER THEIR CARE

We invite your attention to the dangers which at present seem to threaten the female character with wide-spread and permanent injury.

The appropriate duties and influence of woman are clearly stated in the New Testament. Those duties and that influence are unobtrusive and private, but the source of mighty power. When the mild, dependent, softening influence of woman upon the sternness of man's opinions is fully exercised, society feels the effects of it in a thousand forms. The power of woman is in her dependence, flowing from the consciousness of that weakness which God has given her for her protection. . . . There are social influences which females use in promoting piety and the great objects of Christian benevolence which we cannot too highly commend. We appreciate the unostentatious [modest] prayers and efforts of woman in advancing the cause of religion at home and abroad; in Sabbath-schools; in leading religious inquirers to the pastors for instruction; and in all such associated effort as becomes the modesty of her sex. . . .

> *"The power of woman is in her dependence, flowing from the consciousness of that weakness which God has given her."*

But when she assumes the place and tone of man as a public reformer, our care and protection of her seem unnecessary; we put ourselves in self-defence against her; she yields the power which God has given her for protection, and her character becomes unnatural. . . . We cannot, therefore, but regret the mistaken conduct of those who encourage females to bear an obtrusive and ostentatious part in measures of reform, and countenance [approve] any of that sex who so far forget themselves as to itinerate [travel] in the character of public lecturers and teachers. . . . That modesty and delicacy which is the charm of domestic life, and which constitutes the true influence of woman in society, is consumed, and the way opened, as we apprehend [anticipate], for degeneracy and ruin.

—From The Liberator, *August 11, 1837. Reprinted in Judith Papachristou,* Women Together. *New York: Alfred A. Knopf, 1976.*

1. According to the church leaders, what is woman's proper role in society?
2. What dangers does the church associate with women's abolitionist activities?

## Sarah Grimké Defends Female Abolitionists

At first the controversy over their role in public reform deeply troubled the Grimké sisters. As the attacks grew increasingly hostile, however, their self-doubts turned to indignation. Through their speeches and letters, the women defended not only their right to speak out on abolition but also what Angelina termed "the rights of woman as a moral, intelligent and responsible being." In this letter to fellow abolitionist Mary Parker, Sarah answered the Congregational Church's pastoral letter point by point.

7TH MO[NTH] 17, 1837.

Dear Friend, . . . The Pastoral Letter of the General Association . . . says, "We invite your attention to the dangers which at present seem to threaten the FEMALE CHARACTER with widespread and permanent injury." I rejoice that they have called the attention of my sex to this subject, because I believe if woman investigates it, she will soon discover

Sarah (*top*) and
Angelina Grimké

that danger is impending, though from a totally different source from that which the Association apprehends,—danger from those who . . . are unwilling to permit us to fill that sphere which God created us to move in. . . .

The New Testament has been referred to, and I am willing to abide by its decisions, but must enter my protest against the false translation of some passages by the MEN who did that work, and against the perverted interpretation by the MEN who undertook to write commentaries. . . . I follow [Jesus] through all his precepts, and find him giving the same directions to women as to men, never even referring to the distinction now so strenuously insisted upon between masculine and feminine virtues: this is one of the anti-christian "traditions of men" which are taught instead of the "commandments of God". Men and women were CREATED EQUAL; they are both moral and accountable beings, and whatever is *right* for man to do, is *right* for woman.

*". . . whatever is right for man to do, is right for woman."*

But the influence of woman, says the Association, is to be private and unobtrusive. . . . "Her influence is the source of mighty power." This has ever been the flattering language of man since he laid aside the whip as a means to keep woman in subjection. He spares her body; but the war he has waged against her mind, her heart, and her soul, has been no less destructive to her as a moral being. How monstrous, how anti-christian, is the doctrine that woman is to be dependent on man! Where, in all the sacred Scriptures, is this taught? . . .

The General Association say, that "when woman assumes the place and tone of man as a public reformer, . . . her character becomes unnatural." Here again the unscriptural notion is held up, that there is a distinction between the duties of men and women as moral beings; that what is virtue in man, is vice in woman. . . . When [a woman] is engaged in the great work of public reformation . . . she must feel . . . that she is fulfilling one of the important duties laid upon her as an accountable being, and that her character, instead of being "unnatural," is in exact accordance with the will of Him to whom, and to no other, she is responsible for the talents and the gifts confided to her. . . .

*Sarah M. Grimké*

—*From Sarah Grimké,* Letters on the Equality of the Sexes and the Condition of Woman. *New York: Burt Franklin, 1970.*

## THINK ABOUT THIS

**1.** According to Sarah Grimké, how has the Bible been misinterpreted by men in order to suppress women?

**2.** Why do you think many male abolitionists—including some who believed in equality for women—urged the Grimké sisters to drop the women's rights issue?

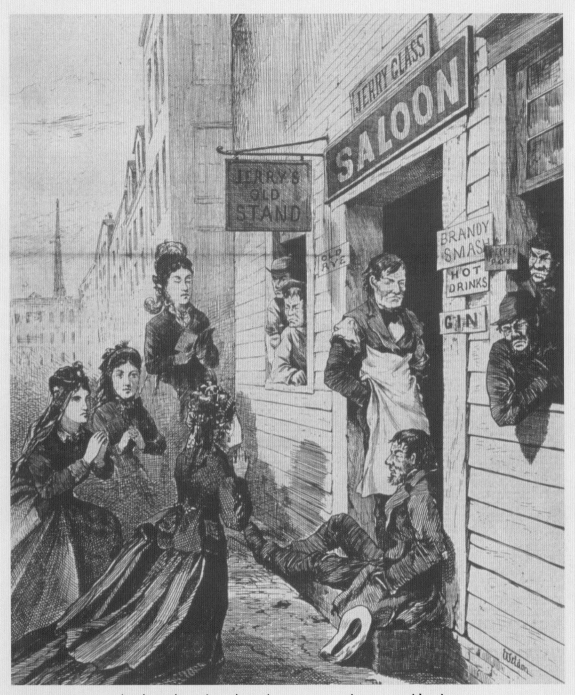

The clientele at this saloon don't seem much impressed by the
temperance ladies praying outside their door. This cartoon appeared
in a New York City newspaper on March 5, 1874.

# Chapter 3

# Crusading Ladies and the Reform Era

THE ABOLITION MOVEMENT took place during an exciting period known as the era of reform. In the early 1800s Americans began to examine their young society. Critics pointed to a variety of social evils and called for change. Besides abolition there were movements to expand education, upgrade hospitals and prisons, and improve working conditions in factories. "Moral reformers" strove to end prostitution and find respectable jobs for "fallen women." Temperance workers campaigned against the use of alcohol. Peace activists called for international courts and congresses, where nations could resolve their conflicts without war.

Women were active in all these causes. Often their involvement in reform movements grew out of their charity work. In small towns and cities across America, women were the backbone of religious and charitable societies formed to aid the poor and raise funds for Christian missionaries. They met in sewing circles to make clothing and other items for the needy. They ventured into poor neighborhoods to distribute food, firewood, household goods, and Bibles. These activities allowed women to step outside the confines of their

In the mid-1800s some women traded their full skirts and cinched waists for "bloomers."

homes, while doing important work approved by their communities and churches.

It was just a short step from helping the victims of social ills to trying to change society itself. While abolition and temperance attracted the majority of female reformers, women also made notable contributions in other fields. Emma Willard and other education pioneers founded the first schools offering young women a chance to study advanced subjects formerly taught only to men. Dorothea Dix investigated American prisons and found the mentally ill housed alongside criminals in squalid cells. Her reports on these horrors led to major prison reforms and the establishment of the first mental hospitals.

Not all reform efforts were successful. One major flop was dress reform. Nineteenth-century women's fashions, which included tight corsets and wide hoop skirts, were uncomfortable and restrictive. When reformer Amelia Bloomer adopted an alternative style featuring baggy trousers worn under a knee-length skirt, many women copied the more practical costume. However, "bloomers" attracted so much ridicule that women soon stopped wearing them.

No matter what cause women championed—from abolition to temperance to "bloomerism"—the reform era provided them with valuable experience. They were expanding their roles, gaining confidence, and forming bonds of sisterhood that would lead to their greatest struggle of all, the campaign for women's rights.

## Emma Willard Calls for Education Reform

A major obstacle to women's advancement was their lack of education. After completing elementary school, only boys could go on to study in America's public secondary schools and high schools. Some girls attended "female academies," where they were instructed in singing, painting, French, and other fashionable subjects. However, the academies charged high tuitions, so they benefited mainly the daughters of well-to-do families.

Emma Willard founded America's first free high school for girls.

Emma Willard believed that women were entitled to the same educational opportunities as men. In this 1819 speech to the New York State legislature, she listed several ways that better female education would benefit both women and society. Willard was seeking funds to establish a public school where girls could study a broad range of subjects, including English literature, music, history, geography, algebra, science, and homemaking skills. The state turned down her request. Two years later, however, the town of Troy, New York, granted Willard funds to open the Troy Female Seminary, America's first free high school for girls. Willard's school paved the way for educators who opened more high schools, the first women's colleges, and the first modern teachers' schools.

**1.** Females, by having their understandings cultivated, their reasoning powers developed and strengthened, may be expected to act more from the dictates of reason and less from those of fashion and caprice.

**2.** With minds thus strengthened they would be taught systems of morality, enforced by sanctions of religion; and they might be expected to acquire juster and more enlarged views of their duty and stronger and higher motives to its performance.

*". . . if housewifery could be . . . taught upon philosophical principles, it would become a higher and more interesting occupation."*

**3.** This plan of education, offers all that can be done to preserve female youth from a contempt of useful labor. The pupils would become accustomed to it . . . and it is to be hoped that both from habit and association, they might in future life, regard it as respectable.

**4.** To this it may be added, that if housewifery could be raised to a regular art, and taught upon philosophical principles, it would become a higher and more interesting occupation. . . .

**5.** By being enlightened in moral philosophy and in that which teaches the operation of the mind, females would be enabled to perceive the nature and extent of that influence which they possess over their children, and the obligation, which this lays them under, to watch the formation of their characters with increasing vigilance.

—*From Emma Willard,* An Address to the Public; Particularly to the Members of the Legislature of New-York, Proposing a Plan for Improving Female Education. *Middlebury, NY: J. W. Copeland, 1819.*

## THINK ABOUT THIS

1. According to Willard, how would better education for women benefit society?
2. How does she reassure critics who feared that education might encourage women to abandon their "proper roles" as wives and mothers?

## A Former "Mill Girl" Recalls a Strike

In the early nineteenth century, industrialization dramatically changed the lives of many American women. The nation's first factories were water-powered textile mills built throughout New England. Thousands of country girls left the farm to work at the mills. They labored fourteen hours a day, six days a week. Their weekly wages averaged two dollars, about half of what male workers earned. At first, working conditions in the mills were fairly comfortable and relaxed. But gradually the factory owners began to cut wages and demand longer hours on speeded-up machines. Workingwomen responded by forming a network of reform associations. These early labor groups staged protests and petitioned state legislatures to pass laws limiting the workday. Harriet Robinson, who began work at age ten at a cotton mill in Lowell, Massachusetts, later wrote about women's entry into the workplace and their efforts to organize.

WE CAN HARDLY REALIZE what a change the cotton factory made in the status of the working women. Hitherto woman had always been a money *saving* rather than a money earning, member of the community. Her labor could command but small return. If she worked out as servant, or "help," her wages were from 50 cents to $1.00 a week; or, if she went from house to house by the day to spin and weave, or do tailoress work, she could get but 75 cents a week and her meals. As teacher her services were not in demand, and the arts, the professions, and even the trades and industries, were nearly all closed to her. . . .

Two mill workers, holding the shuttles they use for weaving cloth, pose for a photo.

At this time woman had no property rights. A widow could be left without her share of her husband's (or the family) property. . . . A father could make his will without reference to his daughter's share of the inheritance. He usually left her a home on the farm as long as she remained single. A woman was not supposed to be capable of spending her own, or of using other people's money. In Massachusetts, before 1840, a woman could not, legally, be treasurer of her own sewing society, unless some man were responsible for her. . . .

One of the first strikes that ever took place in this country was in Lowell in 1836. When it was announced that the wages were to be cut down, great indignation was felt, and it was decided to strike or "turn out" en masse. This was done. The mills were shut down, and the girls went from their several corporations in procession to the grove on Chapel Hill, and listened to incendiary [fiery] speeches from some early labor reformers.

One of the girls stood on a pump and gave vent to the feelings of her companions in a neat speech, declaring that it was their duty to resist all attempts at cutting down the wages. This was the first time a woman had spoken in public in Lowell, and the event caused surprise and consternation among her audience.

*"This was the first time a woman had spoken in public in Lowell."*

—From Harriet H. Robinson, *"Early Factory Labor in New England,"* in *Massachusetts Bureau of Statistics of Labor,* Fourteenth Annual Report. *Boston: Wright & Potter, 1883. Reprinted in Miriam Schneir, editor,* Feminism: The Essential Historical Writings. *New York: Random House, 1972.*

## THINK ABOUT THIS

1. How did the laws and traditions of early nineteenth-century America influence the lives of workingwomen?
2. Why do you think women were a large part of the workforce in the textile mills?

# Amelia Bloomer Publishes a Temperance Newspaper

In the 1830s and 1840s, thousands of temperance societies were organized to combat the excessive consumption of alcohol. Temperance workers ran "abstinence" campaigns, urging men and women to sign pledges promising not to drink. They organized

boycotts of merchants who sold liquor and petitioned lawmakers to regulate or ban alcohol sales. Many women were attracted to temperance, because married women were often the innocent victims of alcoholism. Under the law a wife was powerless to prevent an alcoholic husband from spending all their money, selling their home and property, or abusing her and her children. In 1849 Amelia Bloomer, today remembered mainly for her part in clothing reform, began publishing a temperance newspaper called the *Lily.* In her first issue Bloomer explained women's personal stake in the temperance movement and answered male critics who argued that women should not get involved in public reform.

Temperance leader Carrie Nation

THE FIRST NUMBER of the LILY is to-day presented to its patrons and the public. . . .

It is WOMAN that speaks through the LILY. It is upon an important subject, too, that she comes before the public to be heard. Intemperance is the great foe to her peace and happiness. It is that, after all, which has made her home desolate, and beggared her offspring. It is that above all, which has filled to the brim the cup of her sorrows, and sent her mourning to the grave. Surely she has a right to wield the pen for its suppression. Surely she may, without throwing aside the modest retirement, which so much becomes her sex, use her influence to lead her fellow mortals away from the destroyer's path. It is this which she proposes to do in the columns of the LILY.

*"Intemperance is the great foe to [a woman's] peace and happiness. . . . Surely she has a right to wield the pen for its suppression."*

—*From the* Lily, *January 1, 1849. Reprinted in Judith Papachristou,* Women Together. *New York: Alfred A. Knopf, 1976.*

## THINK ABOUT THIS

1. According to Bloomer, what gives women a special right to work for temperance?
2. What tone does she use in asserting that right? Why do you think she chose to write her editorial in this tone?

## William Lloyd Garrison Answers the "Woman Question"

Throughout the era of reform, the controversy over women's proper role in public life grew increasingly heated. Some of the most impassioned criticism was targeted at women in abolition. William Lloyd Garrison supported full membership rights for women in his New England Anti-Slavery Society. He presented that point of view in speeches and writings, including the following editorial from *The Liberator.* Conservative abolitionists, on the other hand, believed that it was improper for women to speak out or vote in public meetings. Garrison also had opponents who believed in women's rights but wanted to put aside the issue until abolition was achieved. In time the antislavery movement would split in two over the "woman question," with supporters and opponents of women's expanded roles forming separate abolitionist societies.

WE CONTEND THAT THE "woman question," so far as it respects the right or the propriety of REQUIRING WOMEN TO BE SILENT in Anti-Slavery Conventions, when they affirm that their consciences demand that they should speak, is not an "irrelevant" question, but one which it is perfectly proper to discuss in such bodies, whenever the right alluded to is claimed. We are acting, it is true, under an organization for the specific purpose of abolishing slavery; but is it therefore "irrelevant" to inquire how far we may justly go in recognizing the right of woman, as a moral being, to aid us in accomplishing our object? . . .

" *. . . the 'woman question' . . . is not an 'irrelevant' question.* "

There are in our ranks a goodly number of females, who have borne the heat and burden of the cause, who have a keen sense of the woes and wrongs of slavery, and who are as well qualified to deliberate and act in our Conventions, as any of the other sex who are disposed to fetter and gag them. These women, many of them at least, are members of anti-slavery societies, and by the terms of our

Constitution, are entitled to equal rights. Now the question, which as abolitionists, we are called upon to settle, is simply this—*Shall we, when a woman responds aye or no to a proposition which may come before us, or rises, under a conviction of duty, to express her opinion, or to pour out the feelings of her soul in relationship to the unutterable horrors of slavery,* APPLY THE GAG? Shall we tell her on the spot, or virtually by one previous action, TO STOP HER MOUTH? That is the question, and the only question; and it is by no means "irrelevant" to "the specific purpose" of our organization. It is a question, moreover, which must be met and decided, one way or the other.

—*From* The Liberator, *July 27, 1838. Reprinted in Judith Papachristou,* Women Together. *New York: Alfred A. Knopf, 1976.*

## THINK ABOUT THIS

1. In Garrison's view, why should women be permitted to speak out in antislavery meetings?
2. How does he answer the argument that the "woman question" was not relevant to abolition's "specific purpose"?

Elizabeth Cady Stanton gives an impassioned speech during the first women's rights convention, July 19, 1848.

# Chapter 4

# Birth of the Women's Movement

**W**OMEN EMPOWERED BY THEIR WORK as reformers and angered by male domination were speaking out. But isolated protests do not make a movement. To unite, women needed leadership and a program of action. Those essential elements came together at a historic meeting in Seneca Falls, New York.

The seeds for the Seneca Falls convention were planted in 1840, when an international body of abolitionists gathered in London for the World Anti-Slavery Convention. The American delegation included several women. After a heated debate a majority of male delegates voted to bar them from participating. All women attending the convention had to sit in a separate gallery behind a curtain and silently observe the proceedings.

Among the American women outraged by this treatment were Lucretia Mott and Elizabeth Cady Stanton. Mott was the Quaker minister who had helped found the Philadelphia Female Anti-Slavery Society. Stanton was a lively young newlywed visiting London with her abolitionist husband. The two new friends spent hours discussing the question of women's equality and vowed to form a society to work for women's rights.

After they returned home, the women drifted apart. Mott continued her preaching and antislavery work. Stanton tended to the many chores of raising a large family. In her free time she attended abolitionist gatherings. She also helped lead a petition drive that persuaded the New York State legislature to pass the first law granting married women control of their property. Through her hard work in and outside the home, she became increasingly dissatisfied with "the wrongs of society in general, and of women in particular."

In July 1848 Lucretia Mott and Elizabeth Cady Stanton were reunited at a tea party near Stanton's home in Seneca Falls. They were joined by Mott's sister, Martha Wright, and two other Quaker women, Jane Hunt and Mary Ann McClintock. "I poured out, that day, the torrent of my long-accumulating discontent," Stanton later wrote, "with such vehemence and indignation that I stirred myself, as well as the rest of the party, to do and dare anything." By the day's end, the five women had resolved to call a women's rights convention. That assembly launched the first organized movement for women's social and political equality.

Activists in the early women's rights movement worked on a wide variety of issues: legal reform, education reform, dress reform, the right to speak in public, the right to vote. Women also continued to work for other social causes, especially temperance and abolition. In time some of the women active in these reforms would also become feminist leaders. Among the most famous were abolitionists Sarah and Angelina Grimké, Lucy Stone, and Sojourner Truth and temperance workers Amelia Bloomer and Susan B. Anthony.

Susan B. Anthony helped lead the struggle for women's suffrage for more than half a century.

Anthony would play an especially important role in the fight for women's equality. This young Quaker activist first embraced feminism after she was denied the right to speak at a temperance convention. When she and Stanton met in 1851, they became immediate friends and allies. The leadership team they formed would guide the women's movement for the next fifty years.

## Elizabeth Cady Stanton Addresses the First Women's Rights Convention

On July 14, 1848, five women placed a notice in the *Seneca County Courier:* "A Convention to discuss the social, civil, and religious condition and rights of woman, will be held in the Wesleyan Chapel, at Seneca Falls, N.Y., on Wednesday and Thursday, the 19th and 20th of July." Some three hundred people gathered in response. Lucretia Mott, experienced in public speaking through her Quaker ministry and antislavery work, opened the proceedings. Then Mott

Elizabeth Cady Stanton worked for a wide range of women's causes, including suffrage, property rights, and liberalized divorce laws.

introduced Elizabeth Cady Stanton. It was Stanton's "long-accumulating discontent" over the oppression of women that had led to the convention. However, the founder of the women's rights movement had never spoken in public before, and she was terrified. Despite her fears, Stanton gave a passionate speech that held the attention of everyone in the audience.

I SHOULD FEEL EXCEEDINGLY diffident to appear before you at this time, having never before spoken in public, were I not nerved by a sense of right and duty, did I not feel the time had fully come for the question of woman's wrongs to be laid before the public, did I not believe that woman herself must do this work; for woman alone can understand the height, the depth, the length, and the breadth of her own degradation. . . .

Let us consider . . . man's superiority, intellectually, morally, physically.

Man's intellectual superiority cannot be a question until woman has had a fair trial. When we shall have had our freedom to find out our own sphere, when we shall have had our colleges, our professions, our trades, for a century, a comparison then may be justly instituted. . . .

The lamentable want of principle among our lawyers, generally, is too well known to need comment. The everlasting backbiting and bickering of our physicians is proverbial. The disgraceful riots at our polls, where man, in performing the highest duty of citizenship, ought surely to be sober-minded, the perfect rowdyism that now characterizes the debates in our national Congress,—all these are great facts which rise up against man's claim for moral superiority. . . .

*"The right is ours. . . . Have it we must. Use it we will."*

Let us now consider man's claim to physical superiority. Methinks I hear some say, surely, you will not contend for equality here. Yes, we must not give an inch. . . . We cannot say what the woman might be physically, if the girl were allowed all the freedom of the boy in romping, climbing, swimming, playing. . . .

We have no objection to discuss the question of equality, for we feel that the weight of argument lies wholly with us, but we wish the question of equality kept distinct from the question of rights, for the proof of the one does not determine the truth of the other. All white men in this country have the same rights, however they may differ in mind, body or estate. The right is ours. . . . Have it we must. Use it we will. The pens, the tongues, the fortunes, the indomitable wills of many women are already pledged to secure this right. The great truth, that no just government can be formed without the consent of the governed, we shall echo and re-echo in the ears of the unjust judge, until by continual coming we shall weary him.

—From Elizabeth Cady Stanton, Address Delivered at Seneca Falls and Rochester, New York. *New York: Robert J. Johnson Printers, 1870. Reprinted in Ellen Carol DuBois, editor,* The Elizabeth Cady Stanton–Susan B. Anthony Reader. *Boston: Northeastern University Press, 1992.*

1. What arguments does Stanton use to answer the claim that men's superiority over women entitles them to greater rights?
2. What does she expect will be the result of women's demands for equal rights?

The Seneca Falls convention inspired women across the nation to speak out for their rights.

## The Seneca Falls Convention Issues a Declaration

After a day of speeches, the audience at the Seneca Falls convention debated a Declaration of Sentiments. Elizabeth Cady Stanton and the other convention organizers had written the declaration in advance to serve as a public statement of women's grievances and demands. To emphasize the historic significance of their statement, they reached back to the Declaration of Independence. Like that famous document, the Seneca Falls declaration claimed the right to political equality and listed eighteen charges against the "tyrants" who had forced a rebellion. The Declaration of Sentiments also included a number of resolutions calling for an end to women's social, legal, and political inferiority. Most radical was the resolution demanding women's suffrage. During the debates, Stanton argued persistently against opponents who feared that this daring demand would "make the whole movement ridiculous." Finally, after lengthy discussions, the convention passed the suffrage resolution by a narrow margin and approved the Declaration of Sentiments and the rest of the resolutions unanimously.

WHEN, IN THE COURSE OF HUMAN EVENTS, it becomes necessary for one portion of the family of man to assume among the people of the earth a position different from that which they have hitherto occupied, but one to which the laws of nature and of nature's God entitle them, a decent respect to the opinions of mankind requires that they should declare the causes that impel them to such a course.

*"We hold these truths to be self-evident: that all men and women are created equal."*

We hold these truths to be self-evident: that all men and women are created equal; that they are endowed by their Creator with certain inalienable rights; that among these are life, liberty, and the pursuit of happiness; that to secure these rights governments are instituted, deriving their just powers from the consent of the governed. Whenever any form of government becomes destructive of these ends, it is the right of those who suffer from it to . . . insist upon the institution of a new government. . . .

The history of mankind is a history of repeated injuries and usurpations on the part of man toward woman, having in direct object the establishment of an absolute tyranny over her. To prove this, let facts be submitted to a candid world.

He has never permitted her to exercise her inalienable right to the elective franchise [the vote].

He has compelled her to submit to laws, in the formation of which she had no voice.

He has withheld from her rights which are given to the most ignorant and degraded men—both natives and foreigners.

Having deprived her of this first right of a citizen, the elective franchise, thereby leaving her without representation in the halls of legislation, he has oppressed her on all sides.

He has made her, if married, in the eye of the law, civilly dead.

He has taken from her all right in property, even to the wages she earns. . . .

Now, in view of this entire disfranchisement of one-half the people of this country, their social and religious degradation—in view of the unjust laws above mentioned, and because women do feel themselves aggrieved, oppressed, and fraudulently deprived of their most sacred rights, we insist that they have immediate admission to all the rights and privileges which belong to them as citizens of the United States.

*—From Elizabeth Cady Stanton, Susan B. Anthony, and Matilda Joslyn Gage, editors,*
*History of Woman Suffrage, vol. 1. Rochester, NY: Fowler and Wells, 1889.*

## THINK ABOUT THIS

1. Why do you think Elizabeth Cady Stanton placed the denial of women's right to vote first on her list of grievances?

2. Why might supporters of women's rights have considered the demand for the vote too extreme?

## The Rochester Convention
## Adopts Bold Resolutions

Just thirteen days after Seneca Falls, women held a second convention, in Rochester, New York. The Rochester assembly approved the Seneca Falls Declaration of Sentiments and passed even more forceful resolutions. In the following years the two conventions would serve as a model for a series of women's rights meetings held throughout the North and Midwest. Women came together at these conventions to share ideas, pass resolutions, and establish local and state associations to work for reform. Newspaper accounts of their proceedings forced a widening public debate on women's rights. Below are some of the resolutions passed in Rochester.

1. *Resolved,* That we petition our State Legislature for our right to the elective franchise, every year, until our prayer be granted.

2. *Resolved,* That it is an admitted principle of the American Republic, that the only just power of the Government is derived from the consent of the governed; and that taxation and representation are inseparable; and, therefore, woman being taxed equally with man, ought not to be deprived of an equal representation in the Government.

*". . . we deplore the apathy and indifference of woman in regard to her rights."*

3. *Resolved,* That we deplore the apathy and indifference of woman in regard to her rights, thus restricting her to an inferior position in social, religious, and political life, and we urge her to claim an equal right to act on all subjects that interest the human family.

4. *Resolved,* That the assumption of law to settle estates of men who die without wills, having widows, is an insult to woman, and ought to be regarded as such by every lover of right and equality.

5. *Whereas,* The husband has the legal right to hire out his wife to service, collect her wages and appropriate it to his own exclusive and independent benefit; and,

*Whereas,* This has contributed to establish that hideous custom, the promise of obedience in the marriage contract, . . . reducing her almost to the condition of a *slave.* . . .

*Resolved,* That we will seek the overthrow of this barbarous and unrighteous law; and conjure women no longer to promise obedience in the marriage covenant. . . .

*Resolved,* That those who believe the laboring classes of women are oppressed ought to do all in their power to raise their wages, beginning with their own household servants.

*Resolved,* That it is the duty of woman, whatever her complexion, to assume, as soon as possible, her true position of equality in the social circle, the church, and the state.

—*From Elizabeth Cady Stanton, Susan B. Anthony, and Matilda Joslyn Gage, editors,*
History of Woman Suffrage, *vol. 1. Rochester, NY: Fowler and Wells, 1889.*

## THINK ABOUT THIS

**1.** What examples of women's legal inferiority are given in the Rochester Resolutions?

**2.** What specific actions do the resolutions urge women to take?

## Sojourner Truth Gives a "Magical" Speech

One of the most memorable speeches of the early women's rights movement was made by Sojourner Truth. Born into slavery, Truth gained her freedom in 1827 when New York emancipated its slaves. Although she never learned to read or write, she became a famous preacher, abolitionist, and feminist. In May 1851 Sojourner Truth attended a women's rights convention in Akron, Ohio. She listened as a series of clergymen whipped up a group of rowdy men in the audience with lectures on women's physical, intellectual, and moral inferiority. Finally, the six-foot-tall black woman solemnly marched up to the front of the hall and asked the meeting's president, Francis Gage, for permission to speak. Gage later wrote down Truth's speech, noting that its "magical influence . . . subdued the mobbish spirit of the day, and

Sojourner Truth's imposing presence and down-to-earth speaking style drew large crowds to her lectures on abolition and women's rights.

turned the sneers and jeers of an excited crowd into notes of respect and admiration."

WELL, CHILDREN, WHERE THERE IS so much racket there must be something out of kilter. I think that 'twixt the Negroes of the South and the women at the North, all talking about rights, the white men will be in a fix pretty soon. But what's all this here talking about?

That man over there says that women need to be helped into carriages, and lifted over ditches, and to have the best place everywhere. Nobody ever helps me into carriages, or over mud-puddles, or gives me any best place! And ain't I a woman? Look at me! Look at my arm! I have ploughed and planted, and gathered into barns, and no man could head me! And ain't I a woman? I could work as much and eat as much as a man—when I could get it—and bear the lash as well! And ain't I a woman? I have borne thirteen children, and seen them most all sold off to slavery, and when I cried out with my mother's grief, none but Jesus heard me! And ain't I a woman?

*". . . ain't I a woman?"*

Then they talk about this thing in the head; what's this they call it? [Intellect, someone whispers.] That's it, honey. What's that got to do with women's rights or negro's rights? If my cup won't hold but a pint, and yours holds a quart, wouldn't you be mean not to let me have my little half-measure full?

Then that little man in black there, he says women can't have as much rights as men, 'cause Christ wasn't a woman! Where did your Christ come from? . . . From God and a woman! Man had nothing to do with Him.

If the first woman God ever made [Eve] was strong enough to turn the world upside down all alone, these women together ought to be able to turn it back, and get it right side up again! And now they is asking to do it, the men better let them.

Obliged to you for hearing me, and now old Sojourner ain't got nothing more to say.

—From Elizabeth Cady Stanton, Susan B. Anthony, and Matilda Joslyn Gage, editors, History of Woman Suffrage, vol. 1. Rochester, NY: Fowler and Wells, 1881. Reprinted in Miriam Schneir, editor, Feminism: The Essential Historical Writings. New York: Random House, 1972.

## THINK ABOUT THIS

1. What qualities make Sojourner Truth's speech so persuasive and powerful?
2. Why do you think there were close bonds between abolition and the early women's rights movement?

## The *New York Herald* Criticizes "Unsexed Women"

Women's rights conventions provoked an outpouring of criticism. A few newspapers, including the abolitionist press and women's journals such as Amelia Bloomer's *Lily*, supported the women's movement. Most papers, though, called the assemblies shocking and ridiculous. Cartoons and editorials often portrayed the women who attended them as ugly "old maids." This editorial from the *New York Herald* offered a typical blend of outrage and sarcasm.

THE ASSEMBLAGE OF RAMPANT [unrestrained] women which convened . . . yesterday was an interesting phase in the comic history of the nineteenth century.

We saw, in broad daylight, in a public hall in the city of New York,

A cartoonist ridicules the "unsexed women" who joined Elizabeth Cady Stanton and Susan B. Anthony's reform movement.

a gathering of unsexed women . . . publicly propounding the doctrine that they should be allowed to step out of their appropriate sphere, and mingle in the busy walks of every-day life, to the neglect of those duties which both human and divine law have assigned to them. We do not stop to argue against so ridiculous a set of ideas. We will only inquire who are to perform those duties which we and our fathers before us have imagined belonged solely to women. Is the world to be depopulated? Are there to be no more children? . . .

"It is almost needless for us to say that these women are entirely devoid of personal attractions."

It is almost needless for us to say that these women are entirely devoid of personal attractions. They are generally thin maiden ladies, or women who perhaps have been disappointed in the endeavors to appropriate the breeches and the rights of their unlucky lords; the first class having found it utterly impossible to induce any young or old man into the matrimonial noose have turned out upon the world, and are now endeavoring to revenge themselves upon the sex who have slighted them. The second having been dethroned from their empire over the hearts of their husbands, for reasons which may easily be imagined, go vagabondizing over the country, boring unfortunate audiences with long essays lacking point or meaning, and amusing only from the impudence displayed by the speakers in putting them forth in a civilized country.

—*From the* New York Herald, *September 7, 1853. Reprinted in Judith Papachristou,* Women Together. *New York: Alfred A. Knopf, 1976.*

## THINK ABOUT THIS

1. What do you think is the goal of the editorial writer?
2. Why do you think the writer chose to express his opposition to the women's rights movement through personal attacks rather than objective arguments?

# Chapter 5

# War and Division

I N APRIL 1861 THE TENSIONS between North and South erupted in war. The Civil War brought women's rights activities to a halt. In this time of national crisis, most abolitionist and feminist leaders believed that women should put aside their personal concerns. By devoting themselves to the war effort, they would prove their worth as citizens and earn the rights they had been seeking.

American women made heroic contributions during the Civil War. In both North and South, thousands of female volunteers worked as nurses in soldiers' hospitals. Others served the Union and Confederate armies as scouts and spies. An estimated four hundred women disguised themselves as men and enlisted to fight as soldiers.

Women also performed valuable services on the home front. Volunteers in local soldiers' aid societies made uniforms, bandages, tents, bedrolls, and other military supplies. Tens of thousands of women filled jobs left vacant by male workers in factories, stores, schools, and offices. Others shouldered new responsibilities at home. When the men of the household marched off to war, the

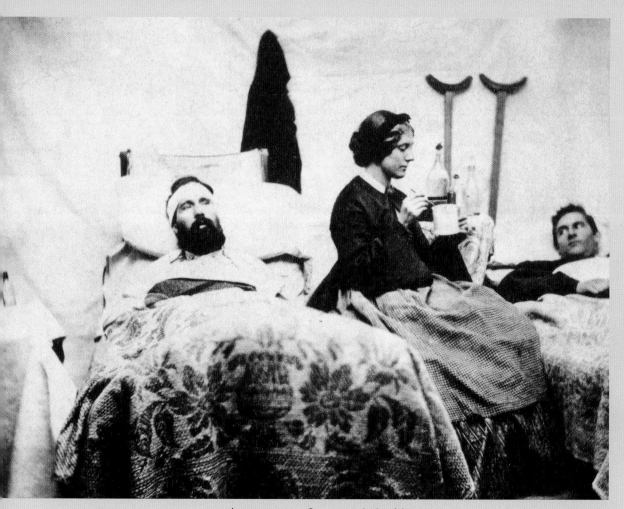

A volunteer cares for wounded soldiers
in a Union army hospital during the Civil War.

Kady Brownell served alongside her husband in the Fifth Rhode Island Infantry.

women they left behind took over the management of farms and businesses, providing for their families in the face of severe shortages, losses, and danger.

Northern women were also active on the political front. The Civil War had begun as a fight to save the Union, but abolitionists were determined to turn it into a war against slavery. To build public support for that broader mission, Elizabeth Cady Stanton and Susan B. Anthony formed the Woman's National Loyal League. Volunteers in the league collected 400,000 signatures on a petition urging Congress to pass the Thirteenth Amendment, which abolished slavery throughout the nation.

In 1865 the Civil War ended. Women who had labored long and hard for their country looked forward to their reward. But they were disappointed. The government remained as reluctant as ever to grant women the vote. Many abolitionists urged women to remain silent a little longer, until the full civil rights of the former slaves had been assured. In the years following the war, women's struggle for equal rights met with one defeat after another. Frustration and disappointment led to bitter disagreements that would divide the women's movement into two opposing camps.

## The Fourteenth Amendment Excludes Women

Shortly after the end of the Civil War, Congress began considering a constitutional amendment to protect the rights of former slaves. The proposed amendment extended citizenship to "all persons born or naturalized in the United States." It also introduced the word "male" into the Constitution for the first time, setting up penalties against states that denied the vote to "male inhabitants" and "male citizens." Women's rights leaders wanted the wording of the amendment changed to include women. Many abolitionists objected. Arguing that this was "the Negro's hour," they warned that combining the demands for black suffrage and women's suffrage would result in defeat for both. Elizabeth Cady Stanton and Susan B. Anthony insisted that women must act at the "open moment," while suffrage laws were being rewritten. They collected 10,000 signatures on the petition reprinted below, urging Congress to consider women's rights. Their campaign ended in defeat. In 1866 Congress approved the Fourteenth Amendment, guaranteeing the full rights of citizenship to men only.

TO THE SENATE AND HOUSE OF REPRESENTATIVES:—

The undersigned women of the United States, respectfully ask an amendment of the Constitution that shall prohibit the several States from disfranchising any of their citizens on the ground of sex.

In making our demand for Suffrage, we would call your attention to the fact that we represent fifteen million people—one-half the entire population of the country—intelligent, virtuous, native-born American citizens; and yet stand outside the pale of political recognition. The Constitution classes us as "free people," and counts us *whole* persons in the basis of representation; and yet are we governed without our consent, compelled to pay taxes without appeal, and punished for violations of the law without choice of judge or juror. The experience of all ages, the Declarations of the Fathers, the Statute Laws of our own day, and the fearful revolution through which we have just passed, all prove the uncertain tenure of life, liberty, and property so long as the ballot—the only weapon of self-protection—is not in the hand of every citizen.

Therefore, as you are now amending the Constitution, and, in harmony with advancing civilization, placing new safeguards round the individual rights of four millions of emancipated slaves, we ask that you extend the right of Suffrage to Woman.

*"... we represent fifteen million people ... and yet stand outside the pale of political recognition."*

*—From a Petition to Congress, 1865. Reprinted in Mari Jo Buhle and Paul Buhle, editors,* The Concise History of Woman Suffrage: Selections from the Classic Work of Stanton, Anthony, Gage, and Harper. *Urbana: University of Illinois Press, 1978.*

## THINK ABOUT THIS

**1.** What arguments does the petition use in its demand for women's suffrage?

**2.** Why do you think the inclusion of the word "male" in the Fourteenth Amendment was a setback for the cause of women's rights?

## Moderate Feminists Concentrate on Women's Suffrage

Lucy Stone, founder of the American Woman Suffrage Association

Southern states quickly found ways to defy the Fourteenth Amendment. It was obvious that further measures were needed to protect African-American voting rights. In February 1869 Congress passed the Fifteenth Amendment, directly prohibiting states from denying the vote to any man on the basis of "race, color, or previous condition of servitude." Again Elizabeth Cady Stanton and Susan B. Anthony protested the exclusion of women. They wanted to oppose ratification of the amendment by the states. A more conservative faction of feminists, led by Lucy Stone and supported by many male abolitionists, agreed to put the urgent needs of the former slaves above women's rights. By late 1869, the issue had split the women's movement in two, with Stanton and Anthony founding the National Woman Suffrage Association and Stone establishing the American Woman Suffrage Association. Over the following decade the two groups would follow different paths in the struggle for women's rights. While the "radical" women of the National demanded changes in many areas of society, Stone's more moderate association concentrated on winning the vote. In this 1870 speech, abolitionist Thomas W. Higginson, vice president of the American Woman Suffrage Association, explained that group's single-minded focus on suffrage.

EARLY IN THE MOVEMENT IN BEHALF of women the broad platform of "woman's rights" was adopted. This was all proper and right then, but the progress of reform has developed the fact that suffrage for woman is the great key that will unlock to her the doors of social and political equality. This should be the first point of concentrated attack. When a fortress is about to be carried by an army, each soldier does not select a separate brick and push at that, but the commander selects one point and concentrates his whole force upon it. Once in, he can dictate his own terms of peace. Suffrage is not the *only* object, but it is the *first,* to be attained. . . . [Our] purpose and aim are to equalize the sexes in all the relations of life; to reduce the inequalities that now exist in matters of education, in social life and in the professions—to make them equal in all respects, before the law, society and the world. Through it we see the end, although it may be afar off. With this burden upon our shoulders we cannot carry all the other ills of the world in addition, we must take one thing at a time. Suffrage for woman gained, and all else will speedily follow. . . . We need not fear that after the accomplishment of suffrage there will be nothing else for us to do before the great end is reached. We are in the work for life, in one form or another. The anti-slavery societies have been dissolved, their work being accomplished, and yet their members find plenty to do. And so we, after we have succeeded in securing suffrage for woman, will join in new movements and carry on the work of progress.

> *"Suffrage is not the* only *object, but it is the* first, *to be attained."*

—*From* The Woman's Journal, *December 3, 1870. Reprinted in Judith Papachristou,* Women Together. *New York: Alfred A. Knopf, 1976.*

1. What reasons does Higginson give for the American Woman Suffrage Association's focus on the single issue of women's suffrage?
2. What does he believe will happen when women win the vote?

## Radical Feminists Seek Broad Reforms

Elizabeth Cady Stanton, Susan B. Anthony, and the other members of the National Woman Suffrage Association were impatient and combative. While conservative feminists hoped to win the vote gradually, by persuading state legislatures to change their laws and constitutions, the radicals demanded a constitutional amendment immediately granting suffrage nationwide. Members of the National also spoke out on a wide variety of other issues affecting women: marriage and divorce laws, working conditions and wages, religion, sex, pregnancy, birth control, abortion. Their attitude was summed up in the motto of their association's newspaper, *The Revolution:* MEN THEIR RIGHTS AND NOTHING MORE; WOMEN THEIR RIGHTS AND NOTHING LESS. This editorial from that controversial paper explained the group's sweeping agenda.

*"The woman question is more than a demand for suffrage."*

WE ARE WHOLLY OPPOSED TO THE . . . attempt to distil our whole great question into a single drop.
The woman question is more than a demand for suffrage. Whoever says it is not, is either a new convert, if a woman, or (more ignorant still) a man. We do not expect men to understand the woman's move-ment—except some solitary, rare spirit here and there. . . . Our chief

## Dr. Mary Walker
### Army Surgeon

Mary Walker, America's first female army doctor, fought for women's rights during and after the Civil War.

### Medal of Honor
### USA 20c

hopes of such clergymen as the Rev. Thomas Higginson is, that when they lend their sacred but clumsy hands to the woman's cause they will not actually mark it with a bruise. . . .

Great as suffrage is in itself, it is only a fragment of the reform on which the hopes of woman depend—a reform whose true foundations do not rest on the surface of her citizenship, but in the heart of her womanhood.

We have said before, and we repeat it with renewed emphasis, that the woman question . . . is a question covering the whole range of woman's needs and demands, woman's rights and wrongs, woman's opportunities and enterprises—including her work, her wages, her property, her education, her physical training, her social status, her political equality, her marriage, and her divorce.

—*From* The Revolution, *November 24, 1870. Reprinted in Judith Papachristou,* Women Together. *New York: Alfred A. Knopf, 1976.*

### THINK ABOUT THIS

1. What reasons does the editorial writer give for the National Woman Suffrage Association's broad definition of women's issues?

2. What points of agreement can you find between this statement and the position of the American Woman Suffrage Association (page 58)?

## Susan B. Anthony Goes on Trial

For more than five decades, Susan B. Anthony worked tirelessly for women's rights, including the right to vote. The feminist leader spent much of her time traveling the country, giving speeches and organizing petition drives. In 1872 she decided to press women's demands for suffrage through a particularly daring action. On election day Anthony led a small group of women to the polling place in her hometown of Rochester, New York. She persuaded the offi-

cials to let them vote. Two weeks later, Anthony was arrested and charged with "illegal voting," a federal crime carrying a possible penalty of three years in jail. She was not permitted to testify at her trial. After her male attorneys presented her defense, Judge Ward Hunt ordered the all-male jury to find Anthony guilty. According to court records,

In later years Susan B. Anthony, who never married, was known as "Aunt Susan" to a new generation of feminists and their children.

the following exchange took place just before the judge pronounced sentence—a one-hundred-dollar fine, which Anthony
never paid.

JUDGE: Has the prisoner anything to say why sentence should not
be pronounced?

ANTHONY: Yes, your honor, I have many things to say; for in your
ordered verdict of guilty, you have trampled underfoot every vital
principle of our government. My natural rights, my civil rights, my
political rights, are all alike ignored. Robbed of the fundamental
privilege of citizenship, I am degraded from the status of a citizen
to that of a subject; and not only myself individually, but all of my
sex, are, by your honor's verdict, doomed to
political subjection under this so-called
Republican government.

JUDGE: The Court can not listen to a
rehearsal of arguments the prisoner's counsel
has already consumed three hours in present-
ing. . . .

ANTHONY: Your denial of my citizen's right
to vote is the denial of my right of consent
as one of the governed, the denial of my
right of representation as one of the taxed, the denial of my right to
a trial by a jury of my peers as an offender against the law, therefore,
the denial of my sacred rights to life, liberty, property, and—

JUDGE: The Court can not allow the prisoner to go on. . . .

ANTHONY: All my prosecutors, . . . not one is my peer, but each and
all are my political sovereigns [rulers]; and had your honor submitted
my case to the jury, as was clearly your duty, even then I should have
had just cause of protest, for not one of those men was my peer; but,
native or foreign, white or black, rich or poor, educated or ignorant,

> *"My natural rights,
> my civil rights, my
> political rights, are
> all alike ignored."*

awake or asleep, sober or drunk, each and every man of them was my political superior; hence, in no sense, my peer. . . .

JUDGE: The Court must insist—the prisoner has been tried according to the established forms of law.

ANTHONY: Yes, your honor, but by forms of law all made by men, interpreted by men, administered by men, in favor of men, and against women.

—*From* The United States of America *vs.* Susan B. Anthony, *Circuit Court, Northern District of New York, June 17–18, 1873. Reprinted in Mari Jo Buhle and Paul Buhle, editors,* The Concise History of Woman Suffrage: Selections from the Classic Work of Stanton, Anthony, Gage, and Harper. *Urbana: University of Illinois Press, 1978.*

## THINK ABOUT THIS

**1.** How does Anthony claim the trial violated her civil rights?

**2.** What is the basis of her demand for women's right to vote?

Students read in the library at Vassar College in Poughkeepsie, New York. Vassar was founded in 1861 to offer women a liberal arts education equal to that provided by the best men's colleges.

# Chapter 6

# Winning the Vote

B Y THE LATE 1800S, the lives of American women were very different from those of their mothers or grandmothers. More girls than ever were graduating high school. Some went on to attend the new women's colleges or men's colleges that went "co-ed," opening their doors to female students. Life also became a little easier for married women, as advances such as packaged foods and new laborsaving appliances relieved some of the endless drudgery of housework.

Taking advantage of their education and their increased leisure time, many women began to explore new horizons outside the home. In 1900 one out of every five women had a job. Millions more joined organizations devoted to cultural, educational, and reform activities. Women's fashions reflected their changing roles. In the late nineteenth and early twentieth centuries, the American woman traded her corset and hoop skirts for a loose-waisted dress with straight skirts, which allowed more comfort and freedom of movement. Newspapers and magazines portrayed this "New Woman" as active, capable, and confident.

Along with all the social changes came advances on the legal front. State by state, the laws were changing to give married women equality in areas such as child custody and the right to control their own wages and property. In one area, though, progress was frustratingly slow—the fight for the vote.

Suffrage workers had won a few early victories on the western frontier. The newly settled territory of Wyoming gave women the vote in 1869, the territory of Utah in 1870. In the 1890s Colorado and Idaho followed. Besides these few gains, however, suffragists had little to show for decades of labor. Year after year they held local, state, and national conventions. They organized state-by-state suffrage drives, lobbied Congress, and pursued their legal claims all the way to the Supreme Court. Women's leaders including Susan B. Anthony of the National Woman Suffrage Association and Lucy Stone of the American Woman Suffrage Association traveled all over the country,

In the early 1900s more women than ever before were working outside the home.

making speeches and coordinating suffrage campaigns.

In 1890 the two women's organizations united to form the National American Woman Suffrage Association (NAWSA). The combined association focused its energies exclusively on voting rights. But the "founding mothers" of the women's movement were beginning to realize that they would not live to see the fulfillment of their long-held dream. "We are sowing winter wheat, which the coming spring will see sprout, and which other hands than ours will reap and enjoy," wrote Elizabeth Cady Stanton shortly before her death in 1902. Susan B. Anthony continued her tireless battle for women's suffrage until her death in 1906.

A fashionable woman at the start of the twentieth century

Capable new leaders carried the suffrage drive through the first two decades of the twentieth century. Carrie Chapman Catt and the hardworking members of the NAWSA won passage of suffrage amendments in twelve additional states. Alice Paul formed the Congressional Union (later the National Woman's Party), a militant group that used controversial tactics such as marches and picket lines to campaign for a federal suffrage amendment. Through the efforts of both moderate and radical feminists, public support for women's suffrage steadily grew.

In June 1919 Congress finally approved a constitutional amendment granting women the vote. The Nineteenth Amendment was signed into law on August 26, 1920. That November, seventy-two years after the Seneca Falls convention first raised the cry for women's rights, millions of American women proudly cast their first ballots.

## Ohio Women Launch a Temperance Crusade

In the late 1800s millions of American women found a "respectable" outlet for their talents and energies in thousands of different clubs and associations. The largest of these new groups was the National Women's Christian Temperance Union (WCTU). The newspaper article excerpted below describes the revival of temperance activities in a small town in Ohio, which led to the founding of the WCTU in 1874. In less than twenty years, the organization would have more than 200,000 members nationwide. Temperance women prayed, marched, and rallied to pressure saloon owners to stop selling liquor and lawmakers to pass prohibition laws. Gradually they also became involved in other social reforms, especially women's suffrage. Laboring side by side with suffragists in state and federal voting rights campaigns, temperance workers lent both numbers and respectability to the feminist cause.

[Following a prayer meeting in Washington Court House, Ohio, on December 26, 1873, a group of women resolved to "go forth" on an "errand of mercy."]

Down the central aisle of the church marched these women to their work, . . . to appeal face to face in their various places of business, to those men who are at work selling liquor. . . .

Thirteen places in all were visited, with the proprietors of which the following exercises were held:

1. Singing; 2. Prayer; 3. Singing; 4. Prayer; 5. Reading of appeal; 6. Promise to call again.

The novel procession created the wildest excitement on the streets, and was the subject of conversation to the exclusion of all other subjects. . . .

Monday, December 29th, 1873.—Promptly at 9 A.M., a still larger attendance at the Presbyterian Church announced that the enthusiasm was still on the increase. . . . A straight course taken for the establishment of Messrs. Anderson and Keller, all the bells in town pealing out a grand anthem of praise. . . .

An ax was placed in the hands of the women who suffered most, and swinging through the air came down with ringing blows, bursting the [liquor barrel] heads and flooding the gutters of the street. One good woman putting her soul into every blow, struck but once for a barrel, splashing Holland gin and old Bourbon high into the air, amid

Temperance leader Carrie Nation described her visits to saloons as "hatchetations."

the shouts of the immense multitudes. Four casks and one barrel were forced open, and the proprietors all the time giving a hearty consent.

—From the Fayette County (Ohio) Herald, *December 1873. Reprinted in Eliza Daniel Stewart,* Memories of the Crusade: A Thrilling Account of the Great Uprising of the Women of Ohio of 1873, against the Liquor Crime. *Columbus, OH: W. G. Hubbard, 1888.*

## THINK ABOUT THIS

1. What do you think is the writer's opinion of the temperance women?
2. Why would the saloon owners give a "hearty consent" to the women's actions?

## A Labor Reformer Speaks Out for Women's Suffrage

Further support for the suffrage movement came from women's labor reform organizations. Groups such as the National Consumers' League (NCL) investigated working conditions in stores and factories. They found women and children working long hours for meager wages in dark, dirty, unsafe buildings. To combat these deplorable conditions, labor reformers campaigned for laws limiting work hours, guaranteeing minimum wages, and regulating child labor. In this speech NCL president Florence Kelley pointed out the connection between working conditions and women's suffrage.

WE HAVE, IN THIS COUNTRY, two million children under the age of sixteen years who are earning their bread. They vary in age from six and seven years (in the cotton mills of Georgia) and eight, nine and ten years (in the coal-breakers of Pennsylvania), to fourteen, fifteen and sixteen years in more enlightened states. . . .

Tonight while we sleep, several thousand little girls will be working in textile mills, all the night through, in the deafening noise of the spindles and the looms spinning and weaving cotton and wool, silks and ribbons for us to buy. . . .

*". . . a girl of six or seven years . . . may work eleven hours by day or by night."*

In Georgia . . . a girl of six or seven years, just tall enough to reach the bobbins, may work eleven hours by day or by night. And they will do so tonight, while we sleep. . . .

Last year New Jersey took a long backward step. A good law was repealed which had required women and [children] to stop work at six in the evening and at noon on Friday. Now, therefore, in New Jersey, boys and girls, after the 14th birthday, enjoy the pitiful privilege of working all night long. . . .

If the mothers and the teachers in Georgia could vote, would the Georgia Legislature have refused at every session

A twelve-year-old spinner in a Vermont cotton factory

for the last three years to stop the work in the mills of children under twelve years of age?

Would the New Jersey Legislature have passed that shameful repeal bill . . . if the mothers in New Jersey were enfranchised? Until the mothers in the great industrial states are enfranchised, we shall none of us be able to free our consciences from participation in this great evil.

—*From "Florence Kelley Speaks Out on Child Labor and Woman Suffrage, Philadelphia, PA, July 22, 1905," at http://www.infoplease.com/ce6/people/a0827309.html*

## THINK ABOUT THIS

1. In Kelley's view, how were all consumers responsible for the "great evil" of child labor?
2. How does she believe women's suffrage would combat that evil?

## The Women's Movement Bows to Racism

The membership of most social reform organizations was overwhelmingly white and middle class. That included the women's rights movement. Many white suffragists—even those who had worked for abolition—shared the racial and class prejudice deeply rooted in American society. To win the support of southern political leaders, they were willing to wink at racist views. Some women's leaders supported educational and financial requirements for voting. Some appealed to southern racists by arguing that women's suffrage would reduce the influence of poor, uneducated black voters. When the National American Woman Suffrage Association held its annual convention in New Orleans in 1903, the group's officers sent this letter to a local newspaper explaining their views on race.

MARCH 18, 1903

To the Editor of the *Times-Democrat:* . . .

Like every other national association, [the NAWSA] is made up of persons of all shades of opinion on the race question. . . . The Northern and Western members hold the views on the race question that are customary in their sections. The Southern members hold the views that are customary in the South. . . .

Individual members, in addresses made outside the National Association, are of course free to express their views on all sorts of extraneous questions, but they speak for themselves as individuals, and not for the Association. . . .

*"The Louisiana State Suffrage Association asks for the ballot for educated and tax-paying women only."*

The National American Woman Suffrage Association is seeking to do away with the requirement of a sex qualification for suffrage. What other qualifications shall be asked for, it leaves to each State. The Southern women most active in the National Association have always, in their own States, emphasized the fact that granting suffrage to women who can read and write, and who pay taxes, would insure white supremacy without resorting to any methods of doubtful constitutionality. The Louisiana State Suffrage Association asks for the ballot for educated and tax-paying women only, and its officers believe that in this lies "the only permanent and honorable solution of the race question."

Most of the Suffrage Associations of the Northern and Western States ask for the ballot for all women, though Maine and several other States have lately asked for it with an educational or tax qualification.

—*From the* (New Orleans) Times-Democrat, *March 1903. Reprinted in Judith Papachristou,* Women Together. *New York: Alfred A. Knopf, 1976.*

## THINK ABOUT THIS

1. What words and phrases does the letter use to reassure racist readers?
2. The letter accepts the idea that each state has the right to impose its own educational and economic requirements for voting. Do you agree with that assumption? Why or why not?

## Suffragists Explain Why Women Need the Ballot

Elizabeth Cady Stanton, Susan B. Anthony, and other feminist pioneers had based their demands for the vote on the Declaration of Independence and women's natural rights. The suffragists of the early twentieth century emphasized more practical concerns. In printed materials such as this flyer distributed by the National American Woman Suffrage Association, they argued that the nation's growing population of workingwomen desperately needed the legal and political protection of the ballot. "I do not want to be governor of the State," said one female factory worker, "but I do want the ballot to be able to register my protest against [working] conditions that are killing and maiming."

JUSTICE                                    EQUALITY

## Why Women Want to Vote.

# WOMEN ARE CITIZENS,

### AND WISH TO DO THEIR CIVIC DUTY.

WORKING WOMEN need the ballot to regulate conditions under which they work.
Do working men think they can protect themselves without the right to vote?

HOUSEKEEPERS need the ballot to regulate the sanitary conditions under which
they and their families must live.
Do MEN think they can get what is needed for their district unless they can
vote for the men that will get it for them?

MOTHERS need the ballot to regulate the moral conditions under which their
children must be brought up.
Do MEN think they can fight against vicious conditions that are threatening their
children unless they can vote for the men that run the district?

TEACHERS need the ballot to secure just wages and to influence the management
of the public schools.
Do MEN think they could secure better school conditions without a vote to elect
the Mayor who nominates the Board of Education?

BUSINESS WOMEN need the ballot to secure for themselves a fair opportunity
in their business.
Do business MEN think they could protect themselves against adverse legislation
without the right to vote?

TAX PAYING WOMEN need the ballot to protect their property.
Do not MEN know that "Taxation without representation" is tyranny?

ALL WOMEN need the ballot, because they are concerned equally with men in
good and bad government; and equally responsible for civic righteousness.

ALL MEN need women's help to build a better and juster government, and

WOMEN need MEN to help them secure their right to fulfil their civic duties.

## National American Woman Suffrage Association

### Headquarters: 505 FIFTH AVENUE, NEW YORK

—From the National American Woman Suffrage Association, May 10, 1910.

1. How does the flyer differ from the Declaration of Sentiments adopted at the Seneca Falls convention in 1848 (pages 43–44)?
2. How are the two documents similar?

## Feminists Send Out Valentines

While members of the National American Woman Suffrage Association labored steadily in state after state to persuade lawmakers to pass suffrage bills, other feminists were growing impatient. Eager to breathe new life into the women's movement, some launched their own independent organizations. Harriet Stanton Blatch, daughter of Elizabeth Cady Stanton, founded the Equality League of Self-Supporting Women (later called

A carload of women and children join a suffragist parade in New York, 1913.

the Women's Political Union). Alice Paul and Lucy Burns launched the Congressional Union (later the National Woman's Party). Radical new organizations such as these tried a variety of inventive techniques to build public and political support for their cause: political lobbying, parades, rallies, demonstrations, billboards, movie-screen advertisements. Some of their actions were highly controversial. Others were simply clever attention getters, like this 1916 campaign to shower U.S. congressmen with prosuffrage valentines.

TO CONGRESSMAN EDWARD STEVENS HENRY,
HOUSE RULES COMMITTEE
    H is for Hurry—
        Which Henry should do.
    E is for Every—
        Which includes women too.
    N is for Now—
        The moment to act.
    R is for Rules—
        Which must bend to the fact.
    Y is for You—
        With statesmanlike tact.

TO CONGRESSMAN THOMAS SUTLER WILLIAMS,
HOUSE JUDICIARY COMMITTEE
    Oh, will you will us well, Will,
    As we will will by you,
    If you'll only will to help us
    Put the Amendment through!

TO CONGRESSMAN EDWARD WILLIAM POU, HOUSE RULES COMMITTEE
The rose is red,
The violet's blue,
But VOTES are better,
Mr. Pou.

*—From Inez Haynes Irwin,* The Story of the Woman's Party.
*New York: Harcourt, Brace, 1921.*

## THINK ABOUT THIS

1. How do you think suffrage opponents might have reacted to these Valentine's Day greetings?
2. Do you think humor can be an effective tool in political campaigns?

## Congress Approves the Nineteenth Amendment

In April 1917 the United States entered World War I. As in previous American wars, women played a large supportive role on both the home front and the battlefront. At the same time, recalling the disappointments of suffragists who put aside their demands during the Civil War, feminists refused to suspend their voting rights campaign. Their efforts now focused on a federal suffrage amendment. Members of the National American Woman Suffrage Association and other moderate women's organizations worked to build state support for the measure. Radical suffragists picketed in front of the White House to protest President Woodrow Wilson's opposition. Finally, Wilson agreed to back the suffragists' cause. The House of Representatives approved the Nineteenth Amendment, also known as the Susan B. Anthony Amendment, in January 1918. The Senate followed a year and a half later. By August 26, 1920, the amendment had been ratified by the states and signed into law.

AMENDMENT XIX

The right of citizens of the United States to vote shall not be denied or abridged by the United States or by any State on account of sex.

Congress shall have power to enforce this article by appropriate legislation.

"The right of citizens of the United States to vote shall not be denied . . . on account of sex."

—From the Constitution of the United States, Amendment XIX. Available online at http://www.archives.gov/national-archives-experience/charters/constitution_amendments_11-27.html

## THINK ABOUT THIS

1. Why do you think it took so long for American women to win the vote?
2. What do you think the vote symbolized for American women? For men?

# Chapter 7

# Between the Waves

SUFFRAGISTS HAD HOPED that winning the vote would mean the beginning of a period of progress and empowerment for American women. Instead, following the passage of the Nineteenth Amendment, the women's movement fell nearly quiet for forty years.

There were several reasons for this decline. Many women were simply exhausted from their long struggle for suffrage and convinced that the battle for equal rights had been won. Some women's groups dissolved. Those that remained active often clashed over goals and tactics now that they no longer had a compelling cause to unite them. In addition, after World War I, a conservative mood swept the country. Disturbed by the horrors of war and the growth of Communism in Russia and eastern Europe, Americans longed for a return to the "good old days." Reformers who continued to press for change were called unpatriotic and un-American. Critics even charged that the "radical" women who campaigned for birth control or minimum wage laws were secretly in league with Communists out to destroy the American way of life.

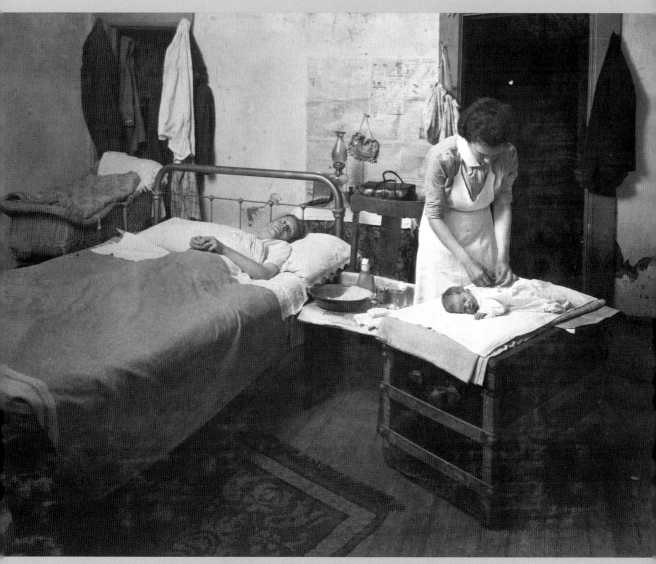

A visiting nurse tends a mother and her newborn baby.
In the early 1900s feminists fought to make
information on birth control available to all women.

Despite all these obstacles, some feminists did continue their struggles for women's rights. The newly formed League of Women Voters worked to educate women about the political process. Alice Paul and the National Woman's Party campaigned for a federal Equal Rights Amendment. The American Birth Control League worked to make contraception legal and widely available. The Women's Joint Congressional Committee, a coalition of women's organizations, pressured Congress to protect workingwomen, poor mothers, and children.

Although these groups scored some small victories, overall the progress was discouraging. By the late 1920s, there had been no improvement in women's wages or working conditions. The few laws that Congress passed to protect workingwomen were over-turned in state legislatures or the courts.

In the 1930s Americans struggled through the Great Depression. During this period of economic crisis and massive unemployment, women who worked were criticized for taking jobs away from men. Many businesses and government agencies refused to hire married women. Even workingwomen who were their family's primary wage earners were routinely paid less than men doing the same jobs.

U.S. entry into World War II in 1941 brought the Depression to a dramatic conclusion. The wartime boom in production also brought startling changes to the lives of American women. During the war, millions of women took jobs in industry, government, transportation, and other traditionally male fields. They enjoyed greater opportunities and better pay than ever before. Women also served in the first female branches of the U.S. armed forces. When the war ended in 1945, however, women in both the civilian and military workforce were expected to surrender their jobs to the returning servicemen.

Many women were happy to resume their time-honored roles as wives and mothers. Others felt deeply dissatisfied. In time their discontent with their place in American society would lead to the rebirth of the women's movement.

## Margaret Sanger Opens a Birth Control Clinic

In the early 1900s federal laws sharply restricted the distribution of information on birth control. Margaret Sanger, who worked as a visiting nurse among poor families in New York City, witnessed firsthand the physical and economic hardships that could result from one unwanted pregnancy after another. In 1913 Sanger traveled to Europe to study government-sponsored birth control clinics. Two years later, she launched a campaign to make contraception widely available in the

Margaret Sanger risked scandal and imprisonment in her battle to legalize birth control.

United States. Sanger published a newspaper and lectured widely on a woman's right to "own and control her own body." She opened the country's first birth control clinic, an event that she described years later in the magazine article excerpted below. Sanger also founded the American Birth Control League, which later became the Planned Parenthood Federation of America. This national organization, with branches across the country, distributed information, supported the development of birth control clinics, and fought to end the legal restrictions on contraception.

IT WAS A CRISP, BRIGHT MORNING ON October 16, 1916, in Brooklyn, N.Y., that I opened the doors of the first birth control clinic in the United States. I believed then, and do today, that this was an event of social significance in the lives of American womanhood. Three years before, as a professional nurse, I had gone with a doctor on a call in New York's Lower East Side. I had watched a frail mother die from a self-induced abortion. The doctor previously had refused to give her contraceptive information. . . .

"... I could not go on merely nursing, allowing mothers to suffer and die."

That night I knew I could not go on merely nursing, allowing mothers to suffer and die. No matter what it might cost, I was resolved to do something to change the destiny of mothers, whose miseries were vast as the sky. . . . The New York State Penal Code declared that only a physician could give birth control information to anyone—and only then to prevent or cure disease. . . . As I was not a physician, I would have no legal protection whatsoever if I gave birth control information to anyone. But I believed that if a woman must break the law to establish a right to voluntary motherhood, then the law must be broken. . . .

We had printed about 5,000 handbills in English, Italian, and Yiddish. They read, "Mothers! Can you afford to have a large family? Do you want any more children? If not, why do you have them?

"Do not kill, do not take life, but prevent. Safe, harmless information can be obtained of trained nurses. . . ."

Would the people come? Nothing could have stopped them!

My colleague, looking out the window, called, "Do come outside and look." Halfway to the corner they stood in line, shawled, hatless, their red hands clasping the chapped smaller ones of their children.

All day long and far into the evening, in ever-increasing numbers they came, over 100 the opening day. Jews and Christians, Protestants and Roman Catholics alike, made their confessions to us. . . .

On the ninth day . . . I was arrested. From the rear of the Black Maria, as we rattled away, I heard a scream. It came from a woman wheeling a baby carriage. She left it on the sidewalk and rushed through the crowd and cried, "Come back and save me!"

**Black Maria**
*police wagon*

—*From Margaret Sanger, "Why I Went to Jail," Together, February 1960.*

## THINK ABOUT THIS

1. Why did Sanger consider the opening of the clinic "an event of social significance"?
2. How did she justify breaking the law by distributing birth control information?

## A Real-Life "Rosie" Joins the Ranks

At the start of World War II, women made up 25 percent of the U.S. labor force. By 1944, that figure had climbed to 36 percent, as five million women answered government's call to "enlist" at their local employment office. Many women found work in fields traditionally reserved for men, including skilled manufacturing jobs in defense plants. They served as riveters (assembling airplanes), welders (heating and joining metal parts), toolmakers, mechanics, steelworkers, and crane operators, for example. Government ad campaigns idealized this new breed of worker as "Rosie the Riveter," a strong, capable, patriotic poster girl whose slogan was "We Can Do It!" Augusta Clawson, a real-life "Rosie," kept a diary of her experiences as a shipyard welder. Like many other women war workers, Clawson found pride and satisfaction in her challenging new role.

> "I've joined the ranks of war workers—I'm going to be a welder in The Shipyard."

WEDNESDAY, APRIL 7 [1943]:

Well, I've done it! I've joined the ranks of war workers—I'm going to be a welder in The Shipyard. It was a sudden decision, and I'm proud of it—I think. But right now, this minute, though I hate to admit it, I'm a bit panicky. . . .

WEDNESDAY [APRIL 14]:

I have completed six days of training, and tonight am the proud owner of two things: one—a black metal lunchbox complete with thermos; two—a firm conviction that I shall become a welder. I've had a few doubts about the latter, wondered sometimes if I could take it. No—that's exaggerated. I knew I *would* be a welder because I'd made up my mind, and I was going to do it or else. . . . But it was mostly a resolve, until now. Tonight I'm sure, because I'm getting such a kick out of it, and because I can see progress. . . .

A World War II defense worker and her poster-girl inspiration, "Rosie the Riveter"

FRIDAY [APRIL 16]:

. . . I am today the proud owner of one check drawn by The Shipyard and payable to one A. H. Clawson, Badge 44651—$20.80 for the three days of last week. I'll have to pay [most of] it over to Uncle Sam [in taxes], but it's fun having it even go through my hands. And I shall keep the stub as a record for posterity. I must have a grandchild, even if I have to adopt one, so I can say, "Darling, in the last war your grandmother built ships." (Probably by then my granddaughter will be an Admiral and won't be impressed at all.)

TUESDAY [APRIL 20]:

. . . My muscles have been forced to develop and harden so rapidly . . . that they are like a watch spring that is wound too tight; they seem to be ready to burst through the skin. It's a queer sensation. You can certainly feel the wheels go round in this hardening-up process.

And it isn't only your muscles that must harden. It's your nerve, too. I admit quite frankly that I was scared pink when I had to climb on top deck today. It's as if you had to climb from the edge of the fifth story up to the sixth of a house whose outside walls have not been put on. Even the scaffolding around the side is not very reassuring, for there are gaps between, where you are sure you'll fall through. The men know their muscles are strong enough to pull them up if they get a firm grip on a bar above. But we women do not yet trust our strength, and some of us do not like heights. But one does what one has to. And it's surprising what one *can* do when it's necessary.

—From Augusta Clawson, *Shipyard Diary of a Woman Welder.*
*New York: Penguin Books, 1944.*

## THINK ABOUT THIS

**1.** What fears did Clawson have to overcome to work as a shipyard welder?

**2.** What benefits did she gain from her wartime work experiences?

## A Workingwoman Prefers Homemaking

At the war's end some women quit their jobs voluntarily. Many others were laid off as factories scaled back and servicemen returned to the workforce. The image of Rosie the Riveter vanished. In its place appeared a new ideal: the full-time homemaker who derived her greatest satisfaction from keeping house, supporting her husband's career, and raising a large family. This image of American womanhood was widely promoted in movies, television, novels, ads, and women's magazines. In 1951 the magazine *Good Housekeeping* printed this article by Jennifer Colton, a young mother who had quit her office job to devote herself to her family. Colton presented a "balance sheet" of the plusses and minuses of exchanging paid employment for full-time homemaking.

### LOST

*The great alibi: work.* My job, and the demands it made on me, were my always accepted excuses for everything and anything: for spoiled children, neglected husband, mediocre food; for being late, tired, preoccupied, conversationally limited, bored, and boring.

*The weekly check.* And with that went many extravagances and self-indulgences. I no longer had the pleasure of giving showy gifts (the huge doll, the monogrammed pajamas) and the luxury of saying "My treat." . . .

*One baseless vanity.* I realize now (and still blush over it) that during my working days I felt that my ability to earn was an additional flower in my wreath of accomplishments. Unconsciously—and sometimes consciously—I thought how nice it was for my husband to have a wife who could *also* bring in money. But one day I realized that my office job was only a substitution for the real job I'd been "hired" for: that of being purely a wife and mother. . . .

> " . . . one day I realized that my office job was only a substitution for the real job I'd been 'hired' for."

### FOUND

*A role.* At first I found it hard to believe that being a woman is something in itself. I had always felt that a woman had to do something

A "happy homemaker"... and her real-life counterpart

more than manage a household to prove her worth. Later, when I understood the role better, it took on unexpected glamour. . . .

*Normalcy.* . . . My relationship with my children is sounder. . . . I realized that when I worked and we had so little time together, we had all played our "Sunday best." The result: strained behavior and no real knowledge of one another.

*Intimacy.* The discovery of unusual and unexpected facets in the imaginations of children, which rarely reveal themselves in brief, tense sessions, is very rewarding.

*Improved Appearance.* Shinier hair, nicer hands, better manicures, are the products of those chance twenty-minute free periods that turn up in the busiest days of women who don't go to business. . . .

*Relaxation.* Slowly, I'm learning to forget the meaning of the word tension. While I was working, I was tense from the moment I woke up in the morning until I fell into bed at night. . . . Sometimes I ask myself, "What would persuade me to go back?" And my answer is, "Barring big medical expenses or a real need for something for the children or my husband, nothing."

—From Jennifer Colton, *"Why I Quit Working,"* Good Housekeeping, *September 1951.*

## THINK ABOUT THIS

**1.** According to Colton, what were the benefits of her decision to quit her job?

**2.** In her view what are some of the good and bad reasons that women work?

# The Kennedy Commission Reports on Women's Status

The picture of America as a nation of blissfully happy homemakers was a myth. In reality, many of the women who lost their jobs following World War II remained in the workforce, settling for lower-paying employment as waitresses, salesclerks, secretaries, maids, or unskilled factory workers. By 1960, women made up 33 percent of the nation's labor force. Their average wages were about 60 percent of what men earned. President John F. Kennedy agreed to a federal investigation of the "prejudices and outmoded customs [that] act as barriers to the full realization of women's basic rights." The report of the President's Commission on the Status of Women confirmed that American women suffered discrimination in areas including employment, education, and the law. It led to the passage of the Equal Pay Act, which required that women and men receive "equal pay for equal work." Because the law excluded workers in a wide variety of fields, however, it had little impact on women's wages. Following are portions of the Kennedy commission report.

### HOME AND COMMUNITY

The Commission recognizes the fundamental responsibility of mothers and homemakers and society's stake in strong family life. Demands upon women in the economic world, the community, and the home mean that women carry on different kinds of activity. Women can do a more effective job as mothers and homemakers when communities provide appropriate resources.

• For the benefit of children, mother, and society, child care services should be available at all economic levels. Costs should be met by fees scaled to parents' ability to pay. . . .

### WOMEN IN EMPLOYMENT

• American women work in their homes, unpaid, and outside their homes, on a wage or salary basis. . . .

• Equal opportunity for women in hiring, training, and promotion should be the governing principle in private employment. An Executive Order should state this principle and advance its application to work under Federal contract.

> "Many of the lowest paid jobs . . . have been filled by women, driven by economic necessity."

### LABOR STANDARDS

Many of the lowest paid jobs in industry and service occupations have been filled by women, driven by economic necessity. They have labored and been exploited as textile and needle trade workers, as laundresses and waitresses, as doers of industrial homework. . . .

In the 1950s waitresses and other workingwomen made about sixty cents for every dollar earned by a man.

• State laws should establish the principle of equal pay for comparable work. . . .

**WOMEN UNDER THE LAW**

Equality of rights under the law for all persons, male or female, is basic to democracy and its commitment must be reflected in the fundamental law of the land. . . . There remain distinctions based on sex which discriminate against women.

—*From* Report of the President's Commission on the Status of Women. *Washington, DC: U.S. Government Printing Office, 1963.*

THINK ABOUT THIS

**1.** What basic assumptions does the report make about women's role in society?

**2.** What are some of the commission's recommendations for actions to combat sex discrimination?

A demonstrator confronts the National Guard in
a 1967 protest against the Vietnam War.

# Chapter 8

# The Second Wave

A CENTURY AFTER ABOLITION LED to the birth of the women's movement, a new age of reform inspired feminism's "second wave." The reforms started with the civil rights movement. African Americans began their struggle against racial discrimination in the early 1950s. Thousands of civil rights activists, both black and white, staged peaceful demonstrations such as sit-ins and marches to demand equal rights and opportunities for all races. By the 1960s, these protests had sparked an examination of many other aspects of society. Young people rebelled against the values of the older generation and experimented with alternative lifestyles. Antiwar protesters opposed U.S. military involvement in Vietnam. Environmentalists, educators, Native Americans, Mexican Americans, and many other groups also challenged traditional beliefs and practices and called for change.

Women were involved in all these reform movements. They battled segregation and helped register black voters in the American South. They marched for peace, picketed industrial polluters, and proclaimed the power of the people to change society. Like the female abolitionists of the nineteenth century, however, twentieth-century women activists found themselves treated like second-class citizens. While men took the leadership roles in protest organizations, women were expected to do the "dirty work." They made coffee, ran errands, answered phones, typed newsletters, and stuffed envelopes. When they objected to their treatment, their concerns were ignored or ridiculed. To one woman volunteer with an environmental group, "Licking stamps began to taste like licking boots."

Women's secondary status in protest movements was a reflection of the continuing inequality of the sexes. In 1965, two years after the passage of the Equal Pay Act, women were still making about sixty cents for every dollar earned by a man. The majority of working women were clustered in low-paying occupations: secretary, typist, salesclerk, waitress, maid. Newspapers listed employment opportunities in two separate categories: "Help Wanted—Men" and "Help Wanted—Women." In many states labor laws, originally written to protect workingwomen, reinforced the discrimination. Women were prohibited from working overtime, starting a business without their husband's consent, or entering occupations deemed too difficult or dangerous, such as firefighting and construction work. In addition, laws and customs often made it difficult or impossible for a woman to borrow money, apply for a credit card, rent an apartment or hotel room, or enter a bar or restaurant without a male escort. Some universities limited women's enrollment. Some barred women from school libraries, for fear they would distract the male students.

The message behind all these measures was clear: Women were the "weaker sex," more dependent and less capable than men. While men were considered the legitimate breadwinners of their households, most people assumed that a woman with a job must be working to earn extra money for luxuries. Young women need not worry about preparing for a career. Instead, they would find fulfillment in their natural feminine roles as wives and mothers.

In the early 1960s women began to challenge these assumptions. Activists pointed out the similarities between women's oppression and the discrimination against African Americans and other exploited groups. Drawing on their experience in protest movements, some women formed their own all-female groups. These organizations worked to examine women's place in society and to fight for freedom from discriminatory laws and practices. A new chapter in the women's rights movement had begun.

The ideal image of the American "housewife" of the 1960s

## Betty Friedan Publishes *The Feminine Mystique*

In the late 1950s journalist Betty Friedan conducted a survey of American women and found that many were deeply dissatisfied with lives that limited them to the role of wife-mother-homemaker. Friedan

Betty Friedan was one of the founding mothers of feminism's "second wave."

published her findings in *The Feminine Mystique.* The book was an instant best seller. By shedding light on "the problem that has no name," it reached out to millions of women who had struggled alone with feelings they were too confused or embarrassed to express. It inspired them to start thinking about the sources of their frustrations and to become aware of unfair laws and practices. Friedan's book had such a huge impact that its publication in 1963 is often considered the start of the second wave of the women's movement.

THE PROBLEM LAY BURIED, UNSPOKEN, for many years in the minds of American women. It was a strange stirring, a sense of dissatisfaction. . . . Each suburban wife struggled with it alone. As she made the beds, shopped for groceries, matched slipcover material, ate peanut butter sandwiches with her children, chauffeured Cub Scouts and

Brownies, lay beside her husband at night—she was afraid to ask even of herself the silent question—"Is this all?"

For over fifteen years there was no word of this yearning in the millions of words written about women, for women, in all the columns, books and articles by experts telling women their role was to seek fulfillment as wives and mothers. Over and over women heard in voices of tradition . . . that they could desire no greater destiny than to glory in their own femininity. Experts told them how to catch a man and keep him, how to breastfeed children and handle their toilet training, how to cope with sibling rivalry and adolescent rebellion; how to buy a dishwasher, bake bread, cook gourmet snails, and build a swimming pool with their own hands; how to dress, look, and act more feminine and make marriage more exciting; how to keep their husbands from dying young and their sons from growing into delinquents. They were taught to pity the neurotic, unfeminine, unhappy women who wanted to be poets or physicists or presidents. They learned that truly feminine women do not want careers, higher education, political rights—the independence and the opportunities that the old-fashioned feminists fought for. . . .

> "Each suburban wife . . . was afraid to ask even of herself . . . 'Is this all?'"

But on an April morning in 1959, I heard a mother of four, having coffee with four other mothers in a suburban development . . . , say in a tone of quiet desperation, "the problem." And the others knew, without words, that she was not talking about a problem with her husband, or her children, or her home. Suddenly they realized they all shared the same problem, the problem that has no name. They began, hesitantly, to talk about it. Later, after they had picked up their children at nursery school and taken them home to nap, two of the women cried, in sheer relief, just to know they were not alone.

—*From Betty Friedan,* The Feminine Mystique. *New York: W. W. Norton, 1963, 1974.*

1. What does Friedan mean by "the problem that has no name"?
2. Why do you think women had difficulty expressing their frustrations with their limited roles and opportunities?

## Title VII Outlaws Sex Discrimination

Many feminists believed that women could win equal rights by working within the political system. They gained a new weapon in their fight with the passage of the Civil Rights Act of 1964. The legislation was meant to eliminate discrimination against African Americans. During congressional debates, a southern legislator who favored segregation tacked on a provision outlawing "sex discrimination," hoping that with the addition, the entire bill would be "laughed to death." To his surprise—and the delight of feminists—the bill passed anyway. Title VII of the Civil Rights Act prohibited job discrimination based on race, color, religion, national origin, or sex. The law would be enforced by a new federal agency, the Equal Employment Opportunity Commission.

**UNLAWFUL EMPLOYMENT PRACTICES**

(a) It shall be an unlawful employment practice for an employer—

(1) to fail or refuse to hire or to discharge any individual, or otherwise to discriminate against any individual with respect to his compensation, terms, conditions, or privileges of employment, because of such individual's race, color, religion, sex, or national origin; or

(2) to limit, segregate, or classify his employees or applicants for employment in any way which would deprive or tend to deprive

any individual of employment opportunities or otherwise adversely affect his status as an employee, because of such individual's race, color, religion, sex, or national origin.

(b) It shall be an unlawful employment practice for an employment agency to fail or refuse to refer for employment, or otherwise to discriminate against, any individual because of his race, color, religion, sex, or national origin, or to classify or refer for employment any individual on the basis of his race, color, religion, sex, or national origin.

*—From Section 703, Title VII of the Civil Rights Act of 1964 (Pub. L. 88-352).*
*Available online at the U.S. Equal Employment Opportunity Commission*
*Web site, http://www.eeoc.gov/policy/vii.html*

## THINK ABOUT THIS

1. What forms of sex discrimination does Title VII prohibit?
2. Why do you think many legislators took seriously the provisions relating to race and religion but treated the inclusion of women as a joke?

## The National Organization for Women Is Founded

Soon after the passage of the Civil Rights Act, it became apparent that the Equal Employment Opportunity Commission had no intention of enforcing the law's sex discrimination provisions. Between 1964 and 1966 women workers filed some four thousand claims of sex discrimination. In nearly every case the commission ruled against them. By June 1966, feminists were fed up. A small group of women led by Betty Friedan decided to form a national organization to work for women's rights. The National Organization

Soon after it was organized, NOW came out in strong support of the Equal Rights Amendment, which had been introduced in Congress back in 1923. In 1972 the amendment finally was approved, but it was never ratified.

for Women (NOW) started out with twenty-eight members and a budget of $140. It quickly grew to become the largest and best known of a series of new women's organizations. NOW used legal and political pressure to fight discrimination against women in the workplace, schools, and government. Its principles and goals were outlined in this Statement of Purpose.

WE, MEN AND WOMEN WHO HEREBY CONSTITUTE ourselves as the National Organization for Women, believe that the time has come for a new movement toward true equality for all women in America, and toward a fully equal partnership of the sexes, as part of the world-wide revolution of human rights now taking place within and beyond our national borders.

The purpose of NOW is to take action to bring women into full participation in the mainstream of American society now, exercising all the privileges and responsibilities thereof in truly equal partnership with men.

We believe the time has come to move beyond the abstract argument, discussion and symposia over the status and special nature of women which has raged in America in recent years; the time has come to confront, with concrete action, the conditions that now prevent women from enjoying the equality of opportunity and freedom of choice which is their right, as individual Americans, and as human beings. . . .

**symposia**
*formal meetings*

We organize to initiate or support action, nationally, or in any part of this nation, by individuals or organizations, to break through the silken curtain of prejudice and discrimination against women in government, industry, the professions, the churches, the political parties, the judiciary, the labor unions, in education, science, medicine, law, religion and every other field of importance in American society.

*—From the National Organization for Women Statement of Purpose, October 29, 1966.*
*Available online at the National Organization for Women Web site,*
*http://www.now.org/history/purpos66.html*

## THINK ABOUT THIS

**1.** What differences and similarities can you find between this statement and the 1848 Seneca Falls Declaration of Sentiments (pages 43–44)?

**2.** What do you think the writers meant by the phrase "silken curtain of prejudice and discrimination"?

## A Quiz Tests Women's "Consciousness"

The majority of NOW's members were white, married, middle-aged, and middle-class. Like earlier feminists, these women fought sex discrimination through traditional channels such as the legislatures and courts. Meanwhile, a growing number of younger women were banding together in independent "women's liberation" groups. These more radical feminists wanted not only to change the laws but to reform society itself, by identifying and eliminating

the sexism at the heart of America's male-dominated culture. A first step in that process was "consciousness raising." In consciousness-raising sessions, small groups of women met to talk about their childhoods, their relationships with men, and the way they were treated at school or work. As they shared their experiences, they realized that many of their personal conflicts and frustrations were really a result of widespread discrimination. Feminist Jayne West developed this quiz as a funny/serious tool to help raise women's consciousness.

Young feminists join a women's rights demonstration in New York's Central Park, 1970.

**TRUE OR FALSE**

1. ___ Woman's work is never done.
2. ___ You can't tell a book by its cover.
3. ___ Housework can be fun.

4. ___ Women make the best mothers.

5. ___ A female dog is referred to as a bitch.

6. ___ One of the more degrading terms that can be
applied to a man is "son of a bitch." . . .

10. ___ The ten most wanted men are men.

11. ___ The opposite of a tomboy is a sissy.

12. ___ Beauty is as beauty does.

13. ___ Intelligent women are often ugly.

14. ___ The best chefs in the world are men.

15. ___ A girl should find out what a man's interests are and learn about
them so as to have more pleasant conversations with him.

16. ___ I can do a pushup.

17. ___ When the blank says check one M_. F_. I do so without
hesitation or contemplation.

18. ___ Some of the finest athletes in the world are women. . . .

22. ___ The way to a man's heart is through his stomach.

23. ___ *Flighty* is often used when referring to men.

24. ___ A permanent isn't really.

25. ___ Gentlemen prefer blondes.

26. ___ I think that it was certainly necessary that the Mormons
had many wives.

27. ___ I often envy the convenience men enjoy in regard to urination.

28. ___ Women are made not born.

> "True or False . . .
> Intelligent women
> are often ugly."

—From Jayne West, "Are Men Really the Enemy?" Reprinted in Rosalyn Baxandall
and Linda Gordon, editors, Dear Sisters: Dispatches from the Women's
Liberation Movement. New York: Basic Books, 2000.

## THINK ABOUT THIS

1. What do you think West hoped to accomplish with this quiz?
2. Do you think your answers might differ from those of a woman taking
the quiz in the 1960s?

# Chapter 9

# Progress and Backlash

B Y THE EARLY 1970s, the women's movement had expanded to include millions of women in hundreds of groups scattered across the country. The divisions within the movement persisted. Members of moderate organizations such as NOW continued to focus on fighting discrimination through the legislatures and courts. Radical feminists called for women's liberation and revolutionary social change. There were also disagreements among women of different racial groups. Women of color often became frustrated because they believed that their concerns were not being addressed by white feminists. Some formed their own independent organizations. Among these were groups of African-American, Puerto Rican, Mexican-American, and Asian-American women.

Throughout the decade feminists in all these diverse groups employed a variety of tactics to pursue their goals. They used petitions, letter-writing campaigns, and lawsuits to force legal reform. They staged strikes, demonstrations, and other actions to call attention to women's oppression. Local groups worked to meet the special needs of the women in their communities. That might include starting a health

Radical feminists march in New York City on
Women's Strike for Equality Day, August 26, 1970.

clinic, day-care center, or self-defense class or pressuring a school or university to fund girls' sports teams or create women's studies programs.

Activists from different organizations often worked together on specific projects. On August 26, 1970, the fiftieth anniversary of the passage of the Nineteenth Amendment, feminists all across the country joined forces to celebrate Women's Strike for Equality Day. Members of women's groups large and small, moderate and radical, took part in the marches and demonstrations held to promote their demands for equality. Other events and issues uniting feminists in the 1970s included campaigns for reproductive rights and passage of the Equal Rights Amendment.

A female volunteer with a fire department in Syracuse, New York

By the end of the decade, the women's movement could point to significant progress. The barriers to women's equal participation in politics, education, and the workplace were beginning to topple. Newspapers could no longer list job openings by sex. State laws barring women from traditionally male jobs such as firefighting and bartending had been overturned. The nation had sworn in its first woman governor (Ella Grasso of Connecticut) and would soon seat its first woman on the Supreme Court (Sandra Day O'Connor). Even the Little League had reformed in response to feminist concerns, reversing its long-standing boys-only policy.

As women celebrated their progress, however, an antifeminist backlash was building. This broad-based conservative crusade would put feminists on the defensive, forcing them to fight to hold on to their hard-won victories.

## The Redstockings Manifesto Rejects Male Supremacy

In 1969 New York City feminists formed an organization called the Redstockings. Like radical feminists in hundreds of other women's liberation groups, the Redstockings called for fundamental changes in American society. Feminists often used consciousness-raising sessions to search for the root causes of women's oppression and come up with solutions. Many groups presented their conclusions in formal statements of principle, or manifestos. The Redstockings Manifesto defined women as an oppressed social class and declared that traditional male attitudes were responsible for their inferior status.

I. After centuries of individual and preliminary political struggle, women are uniting to achieve their final liberation from male supremacy. Redstockings is dedicated to building this unity and winning our freedom.

II. Women are an oppressed class. Our oppression is total, affecting every facet of our lives. We are exploited as sex objects, breeders, domestic servants, and cheap labor. We are considered inferior beings, whose only purpose is to enhance men's lives. Our humanity is denied. Our prescribed behavior is enforced by the threat of physical violence. . . .

> "Male supremacy is the oldest, most basic form of domination."

III. We identify the agents of our oppression as men. Male supremacy is the oldest, most basic form of domination. . . .

IV. Attempts have been made to shift the burden of responsibility from men to institutions or to women themselves. We condemn these arguments as evasions. Institutions alone do not oppress; they are merely tools of the oppressor. . . . Any man is free to renounce his superior position. . . .

We also reject the idea that women consent to or are to blame for their own oppression. Women's submission is not the result of brainwashing, stupidity, or mental illness but of continual, daily pressure from men. We do not need to change ourselves, but to change men. . . .

V. . . . Our chief task at present is to develop female class consciousness through sharing experience and publicly exposing the sexist foundation of all our institutions. Consciousness-raising is not "therapy," which implies the existence of individual solutions and falsely assumes that the male-female relationship is purely personal, but the only method by which we can ensure that our program for liberation is based on the concrete realities of our lives. . . .

VII. We call on all our sisters to unite with us in this struggle.

We call on all men to give up their male privileges and support women's liberation in the interest of our humanity and their own.

—*From the* Redstockings Manifesto, *July 7, 1969. Reprinted in Rosalyn Baxandall and Linda Gordon, editors,* Dear Sisters: Dispatches from the Women's Liberation Movement. *New York: Basic Books, 2000.*

1. According to the Redstockings Manifesto, how are women the victims of male oppression?
2. How does the group believe that women can achieve their freedom?

## Black Women Organize for Action

Relations between white feminists and minority women were often strained. Women of color supported feminist goals such as equal opportunities in education and the workplace. At the same time, they thought that some of the concerns of white feminists were trivial compared to the burdens of racism. As African-American activist Linda LaRue put it, "Blacks are oppressed. White women are suppressed and there is a difference." In the 1970s minority women formed several different organizations to address their needs both as women and as members of a racial community. Black Women Organized for Action, founded in San Francisco in 1973, explained its mission in this membership flyer.

WHO ARE BLACK WOMEN ORGANIZED FOR ACTION?
Old sisters, young sisters, skinny sisters, fat sisters . . . the poor and the not so poor . . . you and me. . . . A bouquet of BLACK WOMEN—action oriented, composed of feminists and non-feminists concerned with the political and economic development of a total Black community. . . .

STATEMENT OF PURPOSE
We are *Black,* and therefore imbedded in our consciousness is commitment to the struggle of Black people for identity and involvement in decisions that affect our lives and the lives of generations of Black people who will follow us.

Coretta Scott King speaks out for minority women at the National Women's Conference in 1977.

We are *Women,* and therefore aware of the blatant waste of the talents and energies of Black women because this society has decreed a place for us.

We are *Organized,* because we recognize that only together, by pooling our talents and resources can we make major change in the institutions which have limited our opportunities and stifled our growth as human beings.

We are *For Action,* because we believe that the time for rhetoric is past; that the skills of Black women can best be put to use in a variety of ways to change the society; that, in the political world in which we live, involvement for Black women must go beyond the traditional fundraising and into the full gamut of activities that make up the political process which affects our lives in so many ways.

—*From Black Women Organized for Action flyer, 1973. Reprinted in Judith Papachristou,* Women Together. *New York: Alfred A. Knopf, 1976.*

1. Why do you think some of the issues raised by white feminists seemed trivial to black women?

2. Why do you think most black women's organizations chose to focus not only on women's issues but on the needs of the entire black community?

## Congress Passes the Equal Rights Amendment

Suffragist Alice Paul introduced the first Equal Rights Amendment (ERA) to Congress in 1923, shortly after the passage of the Nineteenth Amendment. Paul believed that winning the vote was just the first step in the battle for women's rights. The ERA would finish the job by eliminating state and federal laws that supported discrimination on the basis of sex. However, Congress failed to approve the amendment—not only in 1923 but in every year that followed, as women continually reintroduced it. By 1970, the ERA had become a priority for second-wave feminists. Women from many different organizations joined forces to work for its passage. On March 22, 1972, Congress approved the ERA and sent it to the states for ratification.

*Resolved by the Senate and House of Representatives of the United States of America in Congress assembled (two-thirds of each House concurring therein),* that the following article is proposed as an amendment to the Constitution of the United States, which shall be valid to all intents and purposes as part of the Constitution when ratified by the legislatures of three-fourths of the several States within seven years from the date of its submission by the Congress:

Although feminists succeeded in getting the Equal Rights Amendment approved by Congress, it never became a law.

*SECTION 1.* Equality of rights under the law shall not be denied or abridged by the United States or by any State on account of sex.

*SECTION 2.* The Congress shall have the power to enforce, by appropriate legislation, the provisions of this article.

*SECTION 3.* This amendment shall take effect two years after the date of ratification.

*—From the "Equal Rights" Amendment as introduced to Congress in 1971,*
Proposed Amendments to the Constitution of the United States, *Congressional Research Service Report 85–36, Washington, 1985.*

## THINK ABOUT THIS

**1.** Why do you think feminists believed that the Equal Rights Amendment was important?

**2.** What conditions in American society might have led Congress to approve the ERA in 1972 after failing to pass it in previous years?

## The Supreme Court's Decision in *Roe* v. *Wade* Legalizes Abortion

Another issue of great concern to second-wave feminists was reproductive rights. In the 1960s abortion was illegal in most states except under specific medical conditions, for example when the mother's life was in danger. Feminists believed that women should have the right to decide whether or not to have an abortion. In 1970 two feminist lawyers sued the state of Texas on behalf of an unmarried pregnant woman known as Jane Roe, arguing that the laws denying her an abortion were unconstitutional. Dallas district attorney Henry Wade defended the state's antiabortion laws. After a Texas judge ruled in favor of Roe, the defense attorneys appealed the case to the Supreme Court. On January 22, 1973, the Court released its verdict in the landmark case of *Roe* v. *Wade*. By a vote of seven to two, the justices ruled that state laws banning abortion violated a woman's constitutional right to privacy. The decision remains one of the most controversial ever made by the Supreme Court. In his presentation of the majority opinion, Justice Harry Blackmun acknowledged the emotional impact of the abortion issue.

Norma McCorvey *(left)* was known as "Jane Roe" in the historic case that legalized abortion in the United States.

THIS TEXAS FEDERAL APPEAL . . . present[s] constitutional challenges to state criminal abortion legislation. The Texas statutes under attack here are typical of those that have been in effect in many States for approximately a century. . . .

We forthwith acknowledge our awareness of the sensitive and emotional nature of the abortion controversy, of the vigorous opposing views, even among physicians, and of the deep and seemingly absolute convictions that the subject inspires. One's philosophy, one's experiences, one's exposure to the raw edges of human existence, one's religious training, one's attitudes toward life and family and their values, and the moral standards one establishes and seeks to observe, are all likely to influence and to color one's thinking and conclusions about abortion.

> "Our task . . . is to resolve the issue by constitutional measurement, free of emotion."

In addition, population growth, pollution, poverty, and racial overtones tend to complicate and not to simplify the problem. Our task, of course, is to resolve the issue by constitutional measurement, free of emotion and of predilection [prejudice]. We seek earnestly to do this. . . .

**Holmes**
*Supreme Court justice Oliver Wendell Holmes Jr. (1841–1935)*

We bear in mind, too, Mr. Justice Holmes' admonition. . . : "(The Constitution) is made for people of fundamentally differing views, and the accident of our finding certain opinions natural and familiar, or novel and even shocking, ought not to conclude our judgment upon the question whether statutes embodying them conflict with the Constitution of the United States."

—*From* Roe et. al *vs.* Wade, *410 U.S. 113 (1973). Reprinted at the CNN Web site,*
*http://www.cnn.com/SPECIALS/1998/roe.wade/decision*

1. According to Justice Blackmun, what makes the abortion issue so complicated and emotional?
2. How does he describe the Supreme Court's responsibility in deciding the case?

## Phyllis Schlafly Leads an Antifeminist Backlash

Not everyone supported the women's movement. Some critics disagreed with the feminists' support of legalized abortion. Some were turned off by the views and actions of extremely radical feminists. Many conservative Americans were overwhelmed by the social turmoil of the 1960s and 1970s and longed for a return to traditional customs and values. By the mid-seventies, all these concerns had come together in a widespread antifeminist backlash. One of the leaders of the backlash was conservative political activist Phyllis Schlafly. In 1973 Schlafly founded STOP ERA, an organization dedicated to preventing ratification of the Equal Rights Amendment. In speeches and writings such as the following newsletter article,

Phyllis Schlafly led a successful campaign to defeat the Equal Rights Amendment.

Schlafly warned that the ERA would destroy the American family and deprive women of essential protections and privileges. Schlafly's campaign was successful. The deadline for ratification of the ERA was extended to 1982, but when that final deadline was reached, the amendment was three states short of the thirty-eight needed for it to become law.

WOMEN'S MAGAZINES AND TALK SHOWS have been filled for months with a strident advocacy of the "rights" of women to be treated on an equal basis with men. But what about the rights of the woman who doesn't want to compete on an equal basis with men? Does she have the right to be treated as a woman—by her family, society, and the law?

The laws of our 50 states guarantee the right to be a woman—protected and provided for in her career as a woman, wife, and mother. The proposed Equal Rights Amendment will wipe out our laws which guarantee this right. . . .

"... the women's liberationists ... hate men, marriage, and children."

The laws of the 50 states require the *husband* to support his wife and children—to provide a home for them to live in, to protect a woman's right to be a full-time wife and mother, her right *not* to take a job outside the home, her right to care for her baby in her home while being financially supported by her husband. ERA will remove this sole obligation from the husband, and make the wife equally responsible to provide a home for her family and to provide 50 percent of the financial support of her family. . . .

There are two types of women lobbying for the ERA. One group is the women's liberationists. Their motive is radical. They hate men, marriage, and children. They are out to destroy morality and the family.

They look upon husbands as exploiters, children as an evil to be avoided (by abortion if necessary), and the family as an institution which keeps women in "second-class citizenship" or "slavery." . . .

There is another type of woman supporting the ERA from the most sincere motives. It is easy to see why business and professional women support the ERA—many of them have felt the keen edge of discrimination in employment.

To these women we say: . . . the ERA won't give you anything— but it will take away fundamental rights and benefits from the rest of women. You have the right to lobby for the extension of *your* rights— but not at the expense of the rights of *other* women.

—*From* The Phyllis Schlafly Report *6 (November 1972).*

## THINK ABOUT THIS

1. What reasons does Schlafly give for opposing the ERA? Are her arguments emotional, objective, or a combination of both?
2. After reviewing the text of the amendment on pages 113–114, do you find Schlafly's arguments convincing? Why or why not?

An assistant wipes a doctor's brow during surgery.
The women's movement paved the way for the vast numbers of
American women working today in traditionally male fields.

# Feminism Today and Tomorrow

**M**ORE THAN A CENTURY AND A HALF have passed since the birth of the American women's movement. Women have made extraordinary advances in many areas once closed to them. Today women sit on the Supreme Court, serve as ambassadors to other countries, and hold important federal, state, and local government posts. Forty-six percent of the total U.S. labor force is female. That includes increasing numbers of women in traditionally male fields from medicine and law to construction work and truck driving. Laws protect women from discriminatory practices in the workplace, school, and other areas of society.

While all these gains are encouraging, there is still a long way to go before women enjoy full equality with men. Women workers still earn less than men, even when they hold the same jobs. Working wives still bear more than their share of housework and child-care responsibilities. Common assumptions about "masculine" and "feminine" qualities and capabilities continue to limit women's advancement.

Modern-day feminists are working to overcome the lingering forms of discrimination. For many years women's rights activists also had to struggle against the continuing antifeminist backlash. With the success of Phyllis Schlafly's campaign to block ratification of the ERA, newspapers and magazines declared the women's movement dead. Influential conservative groups portrayed feminists as anti-male, antifamily militants and urged a return to "traditional American values." Ironically, the successes of the women's movement also contributed to its decline. In the "postfeminist age," critics argued, American women had it made, especially compared to women in less developed countries. To many people, the women's liberation movement seemed to have become unnecessary and out of step with the needs and values of the majority of Americans.

Shirley Tilghman is the president of Princeton University, formerly an all-male school.

Despite all these obstacles, feminist groups have continued to promote issues of concern to women. In 2006 the National Organization for Women celebrated its fortieth anniversary as the nation's largest women's rights organization, with a membership topping 500,000. Dozens of other groups, large and small, hammer away at a wide variety of issues: the "wage gap"; sexual harassment and assaults; challenges to reproductive rights; child care; the AIDS epidemic; poverty; the image of women in ads, movies, and TV. While the intense activism of the 1960s and 1970s has faded, many feminists believe that the women's movement is in the midst of a thriving "third wave." A nationwide survey conducted for *Ms.* magazine in 2003 found that 83 percent of women and 75 percent of men approved of the movement's goals and accomplishments. A whopping 92 percent of women aged eighteen to twenty-four rated the women's movement favorably. In addition, more women identified themselves as "feminists" than in a similar poll taken eight years earlier.

Even women who reject the feminist label often embrace women's issues in their daily lives—in the way they raise their children, serve their communities, and interact with others at work or school. "Most people bristle at the word *feminist*," says one activist. "It conjures up all sorts of aggressive and abrasive images to them. Do you know how many women will say to me, 'I'm not a feminist, but . . .' And then they'll go on to say every single thing that makes them clearly a feminist."

## Women See a Continuing Wage Gap

In 2005 American women earned an average of seventy-seven cents for every dollar paid to a man—roughly the equivalent of working one week per month without pay. This wage gap is due largely

American women continue to break barriers, performing jobs that were once reserved for men.

to the fact that a majority of women still work in traditionally female fields, with more than half holding sales, clerical, or service jobs. Studies have shown that the more a field is dominated by women or people of color, the lower the pay scale. Even when men and women with similar backgrounds hold identical jobs with the same company, women are still paid less. Women engineers earn about 82 percent of their male colleagues' pay, women surgeons 76 percent, women truck drivers 71 percent. The National Committee on Pay Equity was founded in 1979 to fight sex- and race-based wage discrimination. The organization has campaigned for stronger enforcement of antidiscrimination laws such as the Equal Pay Act. It has also called for new legislation requiring employers to base wages on job requirements such as skill, effort, responsibility, and working conditions, without consideration of race or sex. Finally, the committee works to educate the public about wage discrimination, through publications such as the fact sheet excerpted below.

THE WAGE GAP OVER TIME: IN REAL DOLLARS, WOMEN SEE A CONTINUING GAP

Since the Equal Pay Act was signed in 1963, the wage gap has been closing at a very slow rate. In 1963, women who worked full-time, year-round made 59 cents on average for every dollar earned by men. In 2002, women earned 77 cents to the dollar. That means that the wage gap has narrowed by less than half a cent per year!

"...the wage gap has been closing at a very slow rate."

Over the past 40 years, the real median earnings of women have fallen short by an estimated $523,000—more than half a million dollars.

| YEAR | WOMEN'S EARNINGS | MEN'S EARNINGS | DOLLAR DIFFERENCE | PERCENT |
|------|------------------|----------------|-------------------|---------|
| 2004 | $31,223 | $40,798 | $9,575 | 76.5% |
| 2003 | $30,724 | $40,668 | $9,944 | 75.5% |
| 2002 | $30,203 | $39,429 | $9,226 | 76.6% |
| 2001 | $29,215 | $38,275 | $9,060 | 76.3% |
| 2000 | $27,355 | $37,339 | $9,984 | 73.3% |
| 1990 | $25,451 | $35,538 | $10,087 | 71.6% |
| 1980 | $22,279 | $37,033 | $14,754 | 60.2% |
| 1970 | $20,567 | $34,642 | $14,075 | 59.4% |
| 1960 | $16,144 | $26,608 | $10,464 | 60.7% |

*—From "The Wage Gap over Time: In Real Dollars, Women See a Continuing Gap," © 2004 National Committee on Pay Equity, at http://www.pay-equity.org/info-time.html*

## THINK ABOUT THIS

**1.** Why do you think jobs traditionally held by women and people of color pay less than those held by white men?

**2.** Do you believe that pay equity legislation is necessary and fair? Why or why not?

## Girls Talk about Gender Stereotypes

Girls growing up in America today take for granted many rights that were fought for and won by earlier generations of feminists. At the same time, girls and women still face discriminatory practices and outdated stereotypes that can limit their confidence and opportunities. The organization Girls Inc. recently conducted a nationwide survey of more than two thousand girls and boys in grades three through twelve. The study examined the impact of gender stereotypes on the quality of girls' lives today and their hopes for the future.

| GIRLS' RIGHTS | % OF GIRLS SAYING "VERY IMPORTANT" |

### THE RIGHT TO BE THEMSELVES AND TO RESIST GENDER STEREOTYPES                    86%

60% of girls said that they experience stereotypes that limit this right. 38% said that it is true that "girls are not supposed to be strong and tough." 62% said that "parents want girls to play with dolls not trucks and action figures." 81% said that it is true that "girls are supposed to be kind and caring."

" . . . girls are expected to speak softly and not cause trouble."

### THE RIGHT TO EXPRESS THEMSELVES WITH ORIGINALITY AND ENTHUSIASM            71%

52% of girls said that they experience stereotypes that limit this right. 56% said that it is true that "girls are expected to speak softly and not cause trouble." 51% said that it is true that "people think girls are only interested in love and romance." 47% said that it is true that "people don't think girls are good leaders."

### THE RIGHT TO TAKE RISKS, TO STRIVE FREELY, AND TO TAKE PRIDE IN SUCCESS            59%

49% of girls said that they experience stereotypes that limit this right. 47% said that it is true that "people think girls are weird if they plan to be firefighters or police officers." 44% said that it is true that "the smartest girls in school are not popular." 59% said that it is true that "girls are told not to brag about things they do well."

**THE RIGHT TO ACCEPT AND APPRECIATE THEIR BODIES          72%**

62% of girls said that they experience stereotypes that limit this right. 62% said that it is true that "in school boys think they have a right to discuss girls' bodies in public." 75% said that it is true that "girls are under a lot of pressure to dress the right way." 48% said that it is true that "the most popular girls in school are very thin."

**THE RIGHT TO HAVE CONFIDENCE IN THEMSELVES
AND TO BE SAFE IN THE WORLD          80%**

54% of girls said that they experience stereotypes that limit this right. 63% said that it is true that "girls are under a lot of pressure to please everyone." 65% said that it is true that "girls are expected to spend a lot of their time on housework and taking care of younger brothers and sisters." 33% said that it is true that "people think it is not important to teach girls how to protect themselves."

*—From "Taking the Lead: Girls' Rights in the 21st Century: A Nationwide Survey of School-Age Children Conducted for Girls Incorporated® by Harris Interactive, Inc.," © 2000 Girls Incorporated, at http://www.girlsinc.org/ic/content/HarrisPollBookRev311.pdf*

## THINK ABOUT THIS

1. The study found that older girls were more likely than younger girls to be dissatisfied with gender stereotypes. Why do you think these views changed with age?

2. The study showed that 47% of girls and 29% of boys believed that girls and boys have the same abilities and strengths. What might explain this difference?

# Time Line

**1821**

**SEPTEMBER:**
*Emma Willard opens the Troy Female Seminary.*

**1830s**

**DECEMBER 9, 1833:** *The Philadelphia Female Anti-Slavery Society is founded.*

**JULY 28, 1837:** *The Congregational Church of Massachusetts issues a "pastoral letter" condemning women abolitionists.*

1 8 1 0 s     1 8 2 0 s     1 8 3 0 s     1 8

THE FAMOUS AND ORIGINAL BAR ROOM SMASHER

CARRIE NATION
MANAGEMENT JAMES E. FURLONG

CARRIE NATION

**1840s**

**JUNE 12, 1840:** *The World Anti-Slavery Convention in London votes to exclude women delegates.*

**JULY 19–20, 1848:** *The first women's rights convention is held in Seneca Falls, New York.*

**AUGUST 2, 1848:** *A women's rights convention is held in Rochester, New York.*

**JANUARY 1, 1849:** *Amelia Bloomer begins publishing the Lily.*

**1873**

**JUNE 17–18:** *Susan B. Anthony is tried for "illegal voting."*

40s     1860s     1870s     1890s

**1860s**

**APRIL 12, 1861:** *The Civil War begins.*

**MAY 14, 1863:** *The Woman's National Loyal League is formed.*

**JANUARY 31, 1865:** *Congress passes the Thirteenth Amendment, abolishing slavery.*

**APRIL 9, 1865:** *The Civil War ends.*

**JUNE 13, 1866:** *Congress passes the Fourteenth Amendment, extending citizenship rights to African-American men.*

**FEBRUARY 26, 1869:** *Congress passes the Fifteenth Amendment, protecting the voting rights of African-American men.*

**MAY 15, 1869:** *Elizabeth Cady Stanton and Susan B. Anthony found the National Woman Suffrage Association.*

**NOVEMBER 24, 1869:** *Lucy Stone founds the American Woman Suffrage Association.*

**DECEMBER 10, 1869:** *The territory of Wyoming grants women the vote.*

**FEBRUARY 18:** *The two women's suffrage groups unite, forming the National American Woman Suffrage Association.*

**1890**

MOLLY PITCHER AT THE CANNON'S MOUTH

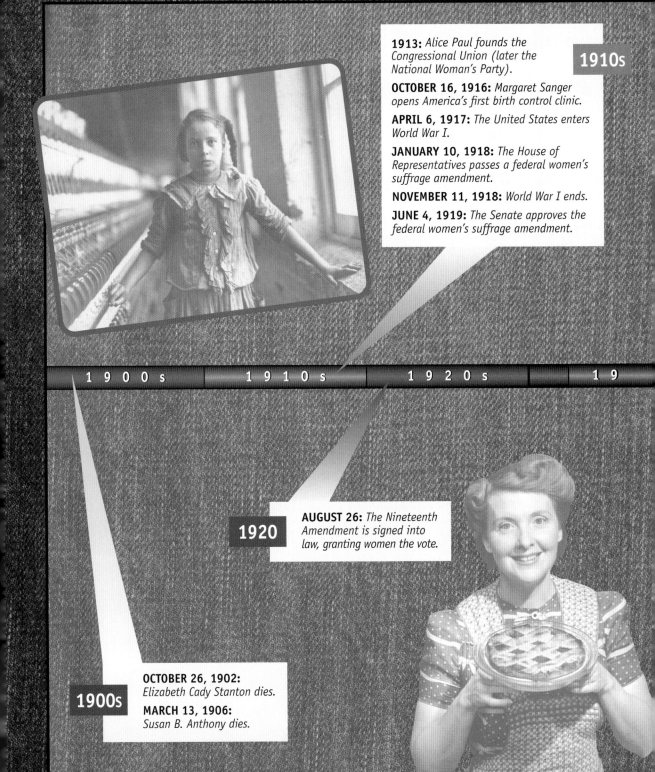

**1913:** *Alice Paul founds the Congressional Union (later the National Woman's Party).*

**OCTOBER 16, 1916:** *Margaret Sanger opens America's first birth control clinic.*

**APRIL 6, 1917:** *The United States enters World War I.*

**JANUARY 10, 1918:** *The House of Representatives passes a federal women's suffrage amendment.*

**NOVEMBER 11, 1918:** *World War I ends.*

**JUNE 4, 1919:** *The Senate approves the federal women's suffrage amendment.*

**1910s**

1 9 0 0 s      1 9 1 0 s      1 9 2 0 s      1 9

**1920**

**AUGUST 26:** *The Nineteenth Amendment is signed into law, granting women the vote.*

**1900s**

**OCTOBER 26, 1902:** *Elizabeth Cady Stanton dies.*

**MARCH 13, 1906:** *Susan B. Anthony dies.*

**AUGUST 26, 1970:** *Feminists observe Women's Strike for Equality Day.*

**MARCH 22, 1972:** *Congress passes the Equal Rights Amendment.*

**JANUARY 22, 1973:** *The Supreme Court's decision in Roe v. Wade legalizes abortion.*

**1970s**

**DECEMBER 14, 1961:** *President John F. Kennedy establishes the President's Commission on the Status of Women.*

**FEBRUARY 1963:** *Betty Friedan publishes The Feminine Mystique.*

**JUNE 10, 1963:** *Congress passes the Equal Pay Act, prohibiting wage discrimination based on sex.*

**1960s**

**JUNE 30, 1966:** *The National Organization for Women is founded.*

**1982**

**JUNE 30:** *The Equal Rights Amendment expires, three states short of ratification.*

4 0 s     1 9 6 0 s     1 9 7 0 s     1 9 8 0 s

**DECEMBER 8, 1941:** *The United States enters World War II.*

**AUGUST 14, 1945:** *Japan surrenders, ending World War II.*

**1940s**

# Glossary

**abhor**  despise

**abolitionist**  a person in favor of abolishing, or putting an end to, slavery

**apathy**  lack of interest or concern

**disseminate**  to spread

**emancipation**  freedom, especially freedom from slavery

**extraneous**  unrelated, not essential

**feminist**  a person who believes in the equality of the sexes

**impunity**  freedom from punishment

**naturalized**  admitted to citizenship; usually refers to a person of foreign birth who becomes a legal citizen of her or his adopted nation

**piety**  religious devotion

**rhetoric**  the art of persuasive speaking or writing; rhetoric can also include fine-sounding but empty words

**suffragettes**  female suffragists

**suffragists**  people who were active in the campaign for women's voting rights

**tenure**  length of time in which a position or right is held

**usurpation**  the act of wrongfully taking something away by force

**vassal**  a person who receives protection from a superior in exchange for loyalty and service

**vehemence**  intensity

# To Find Out More

## BOOKS

Berg, Barbara J. *The Women's Movement and Young Women Today.* Berkeley Heights, NJ: Enslow Publishers, 2000.

Berkeley, Kathleen C. *The Women's Liberation Movement in America.* Westport, CT: Greenwood Press, 1999.

Bolden, Tonya, ed. *33 Things Every Girl Should Know about Women's History: From Suffragettes to Skirt Lengths to the ERA.* New York: Crown Publishers, 2002.

Chipman, Dawn, Mari Florence, and Naomi Wax. *Cool Women: The Thinking Girl's Guide to the Hippest Women in History.* Edited by Pam Nelson. Los Angeles, CA: Girl Press, 1998.

Harness, Cheryl. *Rabble Rousers: 20 Women Who Made a Difference.* New York: Dutton Children's Books, 2003.

Kendall, Martha E. *Failure Is Impossible!: The History of American Women's Rights.* Minneapolis, MN: Lerner Publications, 2001.

Mass, Wendy. *Women's Rights.* San Diego, CA: Lucent Books, 1998.

Monroe, Judy. *The Nineteenth Amendment: Women's Right to Vote.* Springfield, NJ: Enslow Publishers, 1998.

Sigerman, Harriet. *Elizabeth Cady Stanton: The Right Is Ours.* New York: Oxford University Press, 2001.

Stearman, Kaye. *Feminism.* Chicago, IL: Raintree, 2004.

Wheaton, Elizabeth. *Ms.: The Story of Gloria Steinem.* Greensboro, NC: Morgan Reynolds, 2002.

## WEB SITES

The Web sites listed here existed in 2005–2006, when this book was being written. Their names or locations may have changed since then. Use care when using the Internet to do historical research. You will find many attractive, professional-looking Web sites, but proceed with caution. Many sites, even the best ones, contain errors. Builders of Web sites often copy previously published material, good or bad, accurate or inaccurate. In addition, some Web sites promote views of history that responsible scholars reject. Judge the content of *all* Web sites with a critical eye. Always check a site's sponsor or creator. Is it a private individual? An institution or organization? In general, you are most likely to find reliable, balanced information on Web sites that are associated with universities, colleges, or well-known organizations. Compare what you find on the Internet with information from other sources, such as major works of scholarship or reference books recommended by your teachers and librarians. By doing this, you will discover the many versions of history that exist, and you will be better able to weigh different versions for yourself.

*Feminist Majority Foundation Online* at
**http://www.feminist.org**

*Girls Incorporated* at
**http://www.girlsinc.org**

*The Learning Place, National Women's History Project* at
**http://www.nwhp.org/tlp/main/main.html**

*National Women's Hall of Fame* at
**http://www.greatwomen.org/home.php**

*The National Women's History Museum* at
**http://www.nwhm.org**

*Not for Ourselves Alone: The Story of Elizabeth Cady Stanton and Susan B. Anthony,* at
**http://www.pbs.org/stantonanthony/**

*Portrait Monument to Lucretia Mott, Elizabeth Cady Stanton, and Susan B. Anthony,* at
**http://www.aoc.gov/cc/art/rotunda/suffrage.cfm**

*Susan B. Anthony House* at
**http://www.susanbanthonyhouse.org**

*Women's Rights National Historical Park, National Park Service,* at
**http://www.nps.gov/wori/wnhp.htm**

# Index

Page numbers for illustrations are in boldface

## ABOUT THE AUTHOR

"This book tells the stories of American women who struggled against sex discrimination in the schools, workplace, courts, and other areas of society, from colonial times through the present day. These courageous women were patted on the head, ridiculed, insulted, and thrown in jail. They are the reason young girls today can rise as high as their dreams, talents, and hard work can take them. I hope readers will find their stories as enlightening and inspiring as I do."

Virginia Schomp has written more than fifty titles for young readers on topics including dolphins, dinosaurs, occupations, American history, and world history. Her books include one other title in the *American Voices* series, on the Vietnam War era. Ms. Schomp earned a Bachelor of Arts degree in English Literature from Penn State University. She lives in the Catskill Mountain region of New York with her husband, Richard, and their son, Chip.